To Chris
Who we'll miss
Happy Reading

Snippets of a Lifetime

all wishes
Lotte

LOTTE MOORE

First published in Great Britain 2007

A catalogue record for this book is available from the British Library

ISBN 978 0 9550235 4 5

Set in Verdana 10pt

Printed by the Friary Press, Dorchester

Produced by:
YouByYou Books,
Swallow Court,
Dashmonden Lane,
Biddenden,
Kent TN27 8BD.
Tel: 01580 291965
Email: info@youbyyou.co.uk
Website: *www.youbyyou.co.uk*

Contents

Contents continued

Preface

I hope you will all enjoy and share with me the often hilarious, sometimes painful and original experiences that have made me the Lotte I am.

The phases of my journey include childhood, wartime, ballet, the Royal Opera House, acting, marriage, children and now, arrival in old age. There is so much that still inspires me. I have an overwhelming love and interest in children, music and nature, all of which bring me so much pleasure. I'm glad I can laugh at myself too.

I was a willowy girl with long, blonde hair and a calm, sensitive face. I longed to be loved, but all was not well within my fragile capacity to develop. Great unease and insecurity marked my family life. I felt my mother always pushing me away. Others blocked my natural route to her, the *her* that was *my* mother. Other siblings replaced me. I could sense that my great need for affection became a nuisance. I was rescued by dear Granny who gave me the chance to flourish as a dancer at the Royal Opera Ballet.

Soon, immersion in the creative life filled in the emptiness. Amusing incidents in the opera-ballet world taught me to laugh with the pros. Acting introduced me to a vast mixture of characters all of whom gave me something on my journey of survival. It was tough, fun and painful. Marriage appeared most unexpectedly through my love of caring for other people's children. I became a wife and have remained so, through sun and storm, for 35 years.

Nowadays, learning to face my last challenge – accepting old age and all its pain - is like being in a new school for dwindling ancients. Finding courage to face this hurdle will need humour and strength. What better teachers than the young, who rejuvenate me and whom I so love?

The structure of this book is rather unusual. Firstly, I've written my story with me, centre stage. Then comes a series of vibrant Vignettes about the main characters interspersed with a few of my poems.

Finally, there's a series of mini essays called Reflections which are about general topics, thoughts, ideas and anecdotes that don't seem to fit in anywhere else!

Giving birth to this creation has been a very moving, traumatic and therapeutic journey. Often it has provided a safe place for an excessive release of emotions. I've grown in confidence, writing so totally from the heart, yet am not sure how the world will find me or understand this unusual lady.

For Zoë, Daisy and their children. I thank my husband Chris for
his enormous help on the keyboard and Caroline for her caring guidance.
Finally, my profound gratitude to Stephen Rabley who has guided me
through a traumatic journey of memories and realities.
I wrote what follows for my two daughters, Zoë and Daisy, because
I want them to truly know their mum. For Chris, I offer this as a guide
to my past before we met, to celebrate the present and share the future.

*Life is full of choices. We choose who we are, who we love, what we do,
our friends, but we do not choose to be born or when to die.*

My Life

Introduction by a Vampire

As I knelt in a tiny chamber high up inside the huge scaffolding block I heard Roman Polanski shout: "Come up Number 74!" He was way above me on a filming crane. I duly rose from my grave, but my diaphanous dress caught on a nail and I emerged topless.

"Oh shit!" shouted Polanski. "Give her another dress and we'll reshoot."

More hot ice whirled around for misty effect and I was resurrected. Although Polanski had a sharp sense of humour, he wasn't amused by my accident. A near-naked vampire could have caused a riot in the graveyard. It was a boiling hot summer's day in the Hertfordshire fields, sprayed with artificial snow.

Later we prepared for a macabre Vampire Ball. Each of us had a midget partner, who wore an extended nose, which rammed my tummy button as we danced (lucky it wasn't any lower). We wore long fangs which readily popped out when we laughed at the huge balls of garlic hanging everywhere. Many years later, doomed to false teeth, I am more suited to the vampire role (I have only one fang left now!). This was a memorable scene during shooting of *Dance of the Vampires* in 1967, one of many amusing incidents in my eventful lifetime.

Spring 1964

Do you feel it? Can you smell?
There is so much love about even the lampposts
wink at the trees.
The air stands up on its own tickling the branches as
they sigh in the breeze.
Tender love waves from youth and nature's beasts in
provocative beauty chase and yield
Threading new pleasures, luring desire to flourish
as the blossom fills the field
For eyes to feast and hearts to furrow new excitement
in their passionate floods
Surging and swelling, life crackles with a contagious,
brilliant fever of bloods.

Scene 1

Early Days 1936-1949

I was conceived on a houseboat in Kew and born in Maida Vale Nursing Home on 15th March 1936. My mother, Crystal, the eldest daughter of A. P. Herbert, was only 18 and found being a young mother hard. My father, writer and poet John Pudney, decided to have measles before and during my birth. My mother often chided him for the inconvenience of not being there when I was born. They named me Charlotte Anne Pudney.

No doubt being conceived on water, and born a Piscean, has given me a passionate love of water, the sea and the Thames (which I'm lucky enough to live by). There were many times in my turbulent teens when I caught a train to Brighton and sat for hours on the end of the pier writing poetry, talking, crying or sometimes singing to the sea. About 1939 we moved to a wonderful, old farmhouse called Tilty Hill near Great Dunmow in Essex. The house had only just been wired up with electricity. My father soon got to know all the eccentric locals – and became one himself. He loved the countryside.

During our first severe winter I remember the astonished farmers looking at the Pudney children being taught to skate on the duck pond – pushing wooden kitchen chairs across the thick ice to keep our balance. One spring morning the local farmer, Bob, brought a donkey called Bella to see us. She was to prove more unruly than any of us. While Bob was telling Dad about the local blacksmith, Bella trotted across the gravel and entered our front door. Laughing, we hurried after her. Bella was standing in front of the oval, gilt mirror eating our crimson candles. She ate swiftly and purposefully. As we called her she walked round the dining table and backed out of the front door, still munching.

On another occasion, we found her sitting in the drawing room, gazing into the empty fireplace, having devoured a loaf of bread on her way through the kitchen. Only after she ate all the flowers on the piano did we manage to steer her out of the front door.

Later that month our cat called Pilli had a large litter of kittens under the spare room bed in a hat box. It was an exciting introduction to birth, blood, feeding and the facts of nature. Months later when Mummy told us she was going to have a baby, my brother and I rushed out to the dairy and shouted, "Mr Tuke, my mummy is going to have a baby upstairs under the bed in a hat box!" The farmer looked astounded.

My brother Jeremy was two years younger than me. Nanny Sadler, a nursery nurse was engaged to look after him and adored him. She loved dressing him in smart shirts and baby suits. During our first Christmas in church, I remember thinking, *Why do they keep on and on talking about this man called Jesus?* So I stood on the pew during a quiet prayer and called out, "Well, where is this Jesus then? I can't see him." The vicar looked astonished. My mother barked, "Sit, down, Charlotte!" I still haven't seen him – but do pray quite a lot.

In January 1940 a large gang of friendly American soldiers arrived at our house from RAF Debden. A few fields away, a huge, silver barrage balloon was suspended in mid-air. Soldiers slept in squashed rows on the dining room floor. They looked so funny in their striped pyjamas, holding toothbrushes, queuing up for the bathroom in the very early morning. We loved their chewing gum. I remember thinking, *Poor men, they've just missed Father Christmas coming here in the snow.*

Alas, when I was about five years old I was sent to a boarding school, Langford Grove, in Herefordshire. This measure was taken for my safety, although I couldn't understand why it was just me and not all the family who had to go. The school was a huge, old Georgian mansion with vast wooden staircases and log fires, surrounded by glorious countryside and lakes to swim in. Apparently German bombers would never find their way there, it was too peaceful.

I was terrified of two things, matron and fire practice. Firstly, our strict matron squelching along the wooden corridors, appearing suddenly at the dormitory doorway as we sprung in the air, screaming with joy, on our beds, blonde bunches flying and little legs splaying out. Suddenly, Matron's bellow silenced us. It felt life-threatening. The punishment was to lie still for half an hour with our eyes closed.

The second fear, fire practice, was terrible for us tinies. You were devoured by the opening of the sack tunnel, skin was scraped off bent knees and elbows as you gathered speed in the darkness. You descended six floors to land, finally, onto an outstretched blanket and, trembling, into the fireman's arms.

How innocent I was when encouraged to join in the older children's game called Truth, Dare or Promise. I vividly remember being dared to stand outside on a narrow window ledge on the sixth floor, peering down at the gravel drive in terror. How I didn't fall I shall never know. What a cruel test from my elders. I can still feel the dizzy fear, but won wild applause when I fell back into the dormitory.

Another dare, at night time, involved unravelling toilet rolls down four floors of wooden stairs to the hall. How we laughed in our cold dormitory the next morning, when we were kept in for punishment. Luckily we missed the awful ritual of queuing up for daily doses of emulsion (thick, white oily stuff – ugh) and Virol (thick, brown, malty paste – ugh) which used to make me gag. Apparently Virol was full of vitamins for us War children. It was manageable only with the anticipation of bread and dripping at break-time later.

At Tilty Hill in Essex with Mr Took, the farmer and Dad

My brother came to join me at Langford Grove which alleviated my dreadful homesickness a little. In the second month of term he was swinging on an ancient fir tree when he fell and broke his arm. He carried on playing games with it in a sling.

None of us were aware of the dreadful War raging, nor why we should be sent miles away to the safe countryside of Herefordshire. This was indeed a peaceful paradise in which we frolicked naked in the fresh water lakes, found baby owls nesting in the forest and chased each other across acres of grass. The eccentric headmistress, Mrs Curtis, kept us busy and as happy as possible with her carefree approach to life. She made us sit in a vast, wood-panelled room beside a roaring log fire in the evenings while she read us stories.

I don't remember doing any lessons, but recall thick, padded doors behind which the older children practiced piano or other instruments in peace. Often, kindly Mrs Curtis, with her huge, bulging, frog-like eyes, would also play us lovely music.

The school had a long, long drive, so expected parents were eagerly awaited coming round the corner and were met with yelps of joy and excitement. Departure was an elongated pain, accompanied by tears, as it took ages for the cars to disappear.

In 1940-41 the War became more real when Granny took me home at half-term to London. There was no light anywhere. She held her torch low by our feet as we walked home – passing bombed-out houses from which came a strong, sulphurous smell of burning. Granny unlocked the doors of her completely darkened house. Every window was covered with blackout material. It felt a bit like prison. I wanted to see the River Thames at the bottom of the garden, but was forbidden to open the curtains. As I climbed into Granny's huge oak bed I could hear the tugs throbbing past, with their cargoes of wood, coal and produce. Now I began to understand why I had been sent to the country.

After my sister, Tessa, was born - not under the bed - we moved to Kent. Our journey was extremely eventful and noisy because one of the cats had kittens in the back of the car. Bank House was a rambling, Georgian house perched on a steep hill in Chipstead Village near Sevenoaks. Little did we know what thrills we would encounter when two or three inches of snow fell and we zoomed down the empty hill on sledges. No buses were running, so no school. Hooray!

Our three-acre garden hid the secret of vast caves beneath, used by all the villagers as an air raid shelter and which were equipped with blankets, stoves, heaters and food. At the sound of the siren the whole village flocked to the caves, even the sweet-shop lady who was very strict about coupons. I was petrified of the dark and when I descended down the steep, stone steps wearing my red gas mask, I was so scared Hitler would be waiting for us down there.

As a child it was impossible to understand rationing; two ounces of sweets a week, eggs kept in a bucket of water, no butter (only margarine) and having to queue for bread, milk and meat. It was an eerie time for a child. I heard several Doodlebugs passing overhead which, after their engines cut out, fell and exploded on their targets. I wondered who was burning – did I know them?

My father was in RAF Intelligence and often had to fly at short notice. He acquired a highly intelligent Alsatian called Juno as a guard dog for the family. She had a sixth sense of when he was coming home and would sit by the front gate howling, in anticipation of his arrival. Likewise, the day before he went away she would lie disconsolately by the gate. Juno had several litters when she was mated to Wing Commander Peter Wyckham Barnes' huge, handsome Alsatian dog (they were both left in the cellar for the action to take place). The outcome was a litter of eight puppies. We kept one called Bobbie who had one green and one yellow eye, and was sloppy and loving.

The menagerie was further enlarged by Mimi, our white cat. She was a rampant mother, always pregnant, producing several black, some white and one ginger kitten in the frequent births which took place in the next door garden. She would carry each kitten in her mouth over the wall into a shed and lie with them. A flock of white doves also resided in the outhouse. My family of white mice started off in a cage – but often escaped.

Clockwise from top left: with brother Jeremy (right); as bridesmaid to Aunt Lavender; Bank House in Chipstead, Sevenoaks, Kent; with Jeremy at Brighton fish market

On one occasion, our housekeeper Edna was talking to the local baker, Ted, who delivered fresh bread in a huge basket. While they were having a cuddle he felt something move in his pocket, looked down and saw a white mouse jump into his basket to join another one already there inside a tin loaf. Edna screamed, the baker emptied his basket – romance was resumed next day and my white mice giggled all the way back to their cage.

Edna was party to various childhood secrets. After a large Sunday lunch I used to be left at table because I hadn't finished my fatty meat. While the plates were cleared I would tear off the back of *The Times* and wrap up my mouthfuls of chewed meat, put them in my school knicker pocket, race to the kitchen boiler and throw the package into the burning coals. Edna was aware of my dislike for fat of any kind and turned a blind eye.

After Sunday lunch we often had to stand up and recite a poem or act a character that Dad suggested. I remember being in awe of my younger sister reciting all 20 verses of *Sir Patrick Spens* while I could only mimic a garden cabbage singing in the bath.

I went to Walthamstow Hall School for Girls in Sevenoaks. I was an average pupil and absolutely petrified by maths. Our classes were large and I generally managed to get desk 29 or 30 right at the back where the teacher rarely directed questions. I became quite popular in break time by writing the imaginary diary of 'Rochelle', the latest, exciting episodes of which I showed to my friends. When I left at 13 to go to ballet school, Mrs Blackburn, the headmistress, was shocked that I was leaving for such a non-academic career.

Our house was very busy and all sorts of famous people appeared. One day Lord Dunsany and Lord Patrick Kinross were about to sit down for supper when my brother and I swapped the dining chairs around so that Patrick Kinross, a huge, blubbery person, sat on the loose seat and fell through, wedged in the frame of the chair. We rocked with laughter, but Mama was furious.

We disliked Kinross because he always flirted with my mother. He ogled and swooned, almost drooling when sitting next to her.

Another visitor was a lovely, tall, charmer called Sidney Bernstein who eventually founded and controlled Granada TV. He saw us enthralled with a silent Chaplin film and promptly invited us over to his house to meet The Greatest Funny Man on Earth.

Well, it was a bit of an anti-climax, because Chaplin didn't walk with his feet turned out, nor wear *the* hat and, worst of all, when he spoke he didn't sound like the *real* Chaplin. He didn't even have a moustache, but silvery grey hair and a big, happy face. He must have been about 70 then. Of course, there was no TV, so apart from Dick Barton on the wireless, we only saw silent movies.

Make-up games and my brother's Red Hand Gang occupied our lives; our elaborate imaginations creating many adventures in the garden and tree house.

After the European War my father stood as a local Labour candidate for Parliament and I was highly embarrassed seeing him and my mother driving through the crowds with a loud hailer – Mama calling "Vote for Pudney!" - but Dad lost to the Conservatives again.

During the holidays we often visited Chartwell, the Churchills' family home, to swim with Sir Winston and his son Randolph. It was a courtesy to let the PM go in first. One alarming moment occurred when my young brother Jeremy dived underwater and torpedoed Churchill, causing him to splutter and turn turtle. It looked so funny but Mama reprimanded us for laughing. The near sinking of this famous man could have lost us the War. His daughter Mary Soames was a close friend of my mother, so there were many family gatherings.

Malcolm Muggeridge often visited with his two sons. Charlie, the youngest, aroused in me the first murmurings of physical attraction – before my mother ruined his interest. While showing the boys around the house, she got to the bathroom and said, laughing, "Of course, the bath is big enough for two!" Charlie went bright pink. I never saw him again. Sadly, he was killed in an avalanche later.

J.B. Priestley, Dylan Thomas and W.H. Auden often came to dinner. I wasn't there at these raucous parties, but heard the noises from my bedroom. Auden had been at Gresham's with Dad and they both admired each other's verses. Priestley and his wife talked a lot about the locals and their garden. Dylan Thomas was often tipsy.

Two visitors created massive publicity. Guy Burgess and Donald Maclean came to lunch one day and were fascinated by the plot of a book my father was writing called *The Net*, all about spies, subversive plots and treason. They asked my father every detail of the story (he little realising they had plotted to defect to Russia with M15 secrets the very next day). The coincidence was so extraordinary that the press couldn't believe that Dad hadn't known of their plot. Mum and Dad commiserated with Maclean's wife who was devastated at her husband's betrayal of her and their three children, let alone the country.

My dad had a large, detached room, like a long summerhouse, built near the front of our house. It was his study to which he retreated and where he could write uninterruptedly; novels, a series of children's stories and many volumes of poetry. When we returned from school we couldn't just dash in and tell him school gossip, we had to knock or wait till he appeared later. His tiny secretary was called Brightie. She had an almost doglike devotion to Dad, and would accompany him across the road for a lunchtime tipple, return tiddly and be incapable of typing. Her greatest fear was thunder. At the first flash of lightning she would dive under the desk in terror, along with her typewriter, and continue dictation till the storm subsided.

Our family holidays were often spent in France – Dieppe, Varengeville, Rouen and Brittany. Mum spoke fluent French, as well as German.

One year I became ill with a curious ailment that left me lethargic and sleepy for two weeks, so my father nicknamed me Dossey (instead of Dosey), and the name stuck.

My father was a very keen vegetable gardener. We grew everything and Mama helped look after the rose terraces. Dad loved to encourage our discovery of nature and often took us on treks to show us wild mushrooms, a snake skin or the special bark of a tree.

He was therefore mortified one day when Mum asked my brother Jem to go and pick some spinach. He came back with three dock leaves. Another time she told him to bring some asparagus, but my brother returned with a bunch of chopped-off carrot tops.

A Childhood Wish

I had this feeling of longing to fly,
So leapt off the chair and gave it a try.
Arms outstretched I flew round the room
Head held high, I'd be taking off soon,
Mum playing the piano I stood high on a chair,
I flew and I fell with a sickening tear.

Scene 2

Ballet School and the Opera Ballet 1949-1957

When I was about 13, my dear Granny Herbert who was very fond of me as her first-born grandchild, took me to the ballet at the Royal Opera House to see Margot Fonteyn. I had never seen a ballet before and very rarely went to the theatre. I was absolutely spellbound. The experience seemed to release all my emotions. The beauty of Margot Fonteyn's supreme talent filled me with a sudden passion to learn ballet. Granny could see my enthusiasm burning and so she introduced me to Phyllis Bedell who ran her own ballet school in Kilburn.

After persuading my then warring parents that she – Granny – would pay for my dedicated training, she took me to my first boarding ballet school. I was a late starter in a profession which requires arduous training. I slogged so hard. My body was challenged by the great physical strain, but I was enthralled and became utterly dedicated.

Finally, after many exams, I got into the Royal Ballet School – a triumph indeed. There the rigours and discipline under the severe presence of Dame Ninette de Valois were both terrifying and inspiring. Her amazing ability to pluck out talent with one swoop of her stick or lash out at another whose point was a few degrees out, was awesome. She was the queen who commanded this vibrant nest of working ballet bees. How we worked, sometimes for 12 hours a day, surviving only on an apple and cottage cheese.

The rewards were for about four to six girls to be chosen at the end of the year to enter the Royal Ballet Company in the *corps*. At the time, the height of a dancer was limited to 5ft 7ins, as there was a shortage of tall men, many of whom were doing their National Service. Sadly, I realised the competition was too great to get into the company, but I found myself in the Opera Ballet for Verdi's *Aida*.

A fantastic Italian lady called Marguerita Vallman directed this wonderful opera. Most of the opera ballet dancers were very innocent young things, completely unprepared for the sexual innuendos and randy approaches from highly sexed tenors and baritones. Jon Vickers was a most exciting, virile Radames.

During the first big dress rehearsal, as the Grand March started, the Coldstream Guards entered with their spears, heavily made up in No. 7 (a very dark brown body paint), their headgear waving gallantly. As they turned round white, spotty skin and hairy legs were revealed - they had forgotten to put make-up on their backs.

My Feelings As I Danced

Coursing through my veins as I dance
Is the physical reaching out to enhance
The fluid limbs perfecting a pose
Music reflecting the spiralling toes.
The ultimate joy as the whole body moves
Thrilling sensations in faultless curves
Emotion that is so nearly divine
Expressing a beauty that's quite sublime.

At ballet school

"Vot is this crazy army doing?" screeched Marguerita. "Black one side, pink the other! Vot kind of men are you? Go and put the stuff on! We'll rehearse till midnight if necessary!" It was a tradition that the genuine Coldstream Guards were always used in *Aida*, though I don't know why.

One night the Queen and Prince Philip came to see the show. We were told to expect Royalty backstage afterwards. The curtain came down. Prince Philip made a beeline for the scantily clad, slave girls who each curtseyed before he spoke to them. Then the director suggested that Her Majesty might like to see the Royal Box and the auditorium from the stage.

The plush velvet curtains swept up to reveal the Royal Box occupied by a Red Cross nurse scurrying around for a possible souvenir. She ducked down and lay on the floor till the curtains came down. The Royal party found this very amusing.

I later had a fantastic experience in Wagner's *Das Rheingold*. Each of we three Rhinemaidens had to learn the German score phonetically and mime as we danced, while the singers sung in a box hidden under the rock. The surging Wagnerian music compelled us dancers to swim and ride towards the gold. The audience didn't know our secret. Our first rehearsal in the crush bar was unforgettable. As I opened my mouth to mime the aria, a fantastic sound exploded in the room. It was Joan Sutherland's debut at Covent Garden. What a glorious sensation to open my mouth, *"via viya..."* and hear my double's soaring voice rise ever upwards. Marjorie Thomas and Elsie Morrison were the other two Rhinemaiden doubles. Joan Sutherland would rock with laughter, causing the rehearsals to stop. She had a wonderful, contagious cackle which ricocheted through the orchestra.

Being fairly naïve dancers we hadn't reckoned with the male passions. Ottaker Kraus, an excellent, but rather ugly singer, played Albrecht seeking to snatch the gold. Poor Lois – a Rhinemaiden – was plagued by his amorous advances. When singing a duet he would pluck at her rubber seaweed, his hands rolling seductively round her pert breasts. The public thought this was all good acting, but Lois, an innocent Lancashire girl, was left with torn costumes every night after he'd passionately kissed her, and was horrified. It was a glorious feeling to swim behind gauze to the wonderful Wagnerian music.

Another eventful rehearsal occurred in *The Carmelites*, a rarely performed opera by Poulenc, about a convent full of nuns who are eventually executed on the scaffold (which they reach by crossing a bridge). The composer creates an eerie single clunk for each nun as the guillotine comes down off-stage. During an arduous rehearsal one evening, at the climax of the opera, the nuns suddenly started disappearing. The music continued. Marguerita Vallman called out, "Ver are ze nuns?"

One appeared on the bridge, saying, "It's past 10pm. Our union says we have to stop now." Marguerita was astounded and filled with rage. "How can you do this - damn your union! Come back all of you, we work till morning like in Italy!"

Below right: on the banks of the Thames; below left: in the studio

Above: in Wagner's Das Rhinegold; *Lois (left), Lotte (centre), Romayne (right) and Joan Sutherland behind gauze*

I played a silent role: when the Sister (Joan Sutherland) was singing of dangerous news I was meant to faint. On the first night, draped round a heavy, mahogany chair, I did the faint, bringing the huge chair down too with a loud clatter, which rather spoilt Joan's aria. What a noisy nun!

I remember too when the Queen came backstage, primarily to meet the great prima donna, Maria Callas, who was wearing a very tight, pencil-thin, long black dress. As all the singers lined up to meet Her Majesty, the Queen held out her gloved hand to Maria Callas who sank slowly into a deep curtsey, splitting her dress right down the back. With fury she flounced off stage, uttering angry words in Italian, leaving the Queen with outstretched hand, a little shocked at such temperament.

During my wonderfully fulfilled time at the Royal Opera House, Romayne, the ballet mistress, met Gregory, a Bulgarian overseas broadcaster at my 18th birthday party (held at Walpole House in Chiswick Mall). There was a hugely embarrassing moment when the debonair actor Michael Dennison asked me to dance. Swirling round in my white organza dress, I noticed little cotton wool balls on the highly polished parquet floor which had escaped from the padding in my dress. As Michael held me closer he dented the inner cups of the fallen falsies. I bent down to retrieve them, blushing, as my mother swept Michael away to get him a brandy and dance with him herself.

Meanwhile Greg was relating his great escape from occupied Bulgaria during the War with another friend Michael Padev. Romayne was entranced by this larger-than-life character. My father and Greg used to have lively political discussions which got so excitable that Greg would eat with his fingers, gesticulating wildly to emphasise a point. Romayne had many happy, crazy years married to him before he died. She was 80 in September 2006 and we went to a wonderful celebration in the Crush Bar of The Royal Opera House. Many well known artists and most of the management cheered her for her teaching and performances over the years. She was in *Nutcracker* in 2006 and when Chris took me to see *Romeo and Juliet* on my 70th birthday I suddenly recognised her playing a court lady. She often used to play a regal Lady Capulet, and has just got a cameo part in 2007 as the housekeeper in *Il Travatore*. In 2006 she choreographed the dancers for Boris Gudonov in Monte Carlo. Her varied roles have covered opera, ballet and modern dance, she is an excellent teacher of all ages and a dear friend.

Sadly, the time came to leave the Royal Opera Ballet. I waited alone one last night on the empty stage of that unique, glorious Opera House. The kind stage doorman, Bill, came to comfort me, and finally led me off the stage through empty corridors (locking up as he went), as I said goodbye to all I had known there. Bill drove me home, sobbing. The extraordinary aura of being in the Opera House, let alone performing, left me with the most wonderful memories of my life. If there is another world, I'd love to rejoin the Opera Ballet in heaven!

In The Belle of New York

Scene 3

My Acting Career 1957-1961

Later in 1957 I was sent on holiday to stay with Dom Mintoff, the Prime Minister of Malta. I had never been in a plane before. As I looked out onto the wings I screamed, "Fire!" The stewardess calmed my terror, explaining it was the exhaust from the engines. My father hadn't realised what an ordeal flying alone would be the first time. I became firm friends with Dom's wife, Millie. She had a difficult life with this flamboyant and eccentric man and poured out her troubles to me.

While in the Opera Ballet I was living in Islington with my mother and her new husband Lionel Hale, the broadcaster and writer, plus his two children, James and Tory, and my brother and sister. I kept up a close friendship with James, even after we both married. Chris and he enjoyed many a literary discussion. Tory, alas, moved abroad, so we didn't see her much. The marriage added new problems to the already difficult relationship with my mother, a forceful, dominant character, who had no room for me in her emotions.

One of the most traumatic events was being given a bedroom next door to Mum. I lay awake, disgusted and revolted, hearing my mother's moans of ecstasy with the man who had taken my father's place. I could tell no one and used to flee downstairs waiting for them to finish. Eventually, I was tolerated no more and sent to live with dear Granny and Grandpa in Hammersmith, where my highly sensitive temperament was understood and loved.

After some training in acting and singing, I was employed in a group doing a review in Amsterdam. The sketches included some amusing songs, one of which was called *Damp Shoes* in which I became a medieval, grand lady sitting on a throne, with little on and soaking feet. We arrived in Holland and went to our tiny hostel. The next morning we looked aghast at our dull breakfast of slices of ham, other cold meats, dry toast and Gouda cheese.

One day I had dreadful toothache and was sent to what I thought was the dentist. Not speaking the language, I found it hard to keep opening my mouth when the white-coated man kept pointing to my feet, finally taking my sock off and taking a scalpel to my toe. I yelled, and left the chiropodist in search of a true dentist.

I cannot remember why I changed my surname to Selwyn, except that it looked better on the credits and was Grandpa's family name. I didn't realise until much later how much it upset my father.

Back in England, I auditioned for *The Snow Goose* pantomime in Brighton and got the part of a paper doily in the ballet. I was also given the understudy part of principal boy, little knowing what was about to happen. Only a day or two before the first performance the principal developed acute appendicitis and was rushed to hospital. On the opening night I was about to say my first words on stage: "Oh, Mother Goose, you do look hot and cross today," to which the Goose would make a grunting noise. I was shaking with fear, not understanding why the audience was laughing, until I saw the golden egg the Goose had dropped begin rolling downstage, in line with the vigorous conductor. I ran to pick up the egg and the Goose hissed, "Leave it there, you fool." I had had virtually no rehearsals.

The previous night I had been walking along the seafront with Jane, my friend, who coached me in the many lines I had to learn. As we strolled along a car stopped and a voice called out, "'Ere, what are you doing out at one in the morning? You'd better get in and explain yourselves." It was a police patrol car, obviously thinking we were Brighton Belle prostitutes looking for business. We explained about Mother Goose and they kindly took us home.

So I made headlines in the Brighton *Argus*: "Charlotte Selwyn steps in to save the show". I also had to perform all the ballet scenes, and then change into a fishnet-stockinged, velvet-waistcoated boy which is how I appeared on stage for most of the show. The stars, Richard Hearne and Dick Emery, were not very helpful, constantly changing their gags around me. But Mother Goose never dropped an egg again. Pantomime in those days was a rough way of learning many professional skills quickly.

My next job was in *Alice in Wonderland* at the Winter Garden in London, playing Lorinna, Alice's sister. The Mad Hatter was Frankie Howerd and Richard Goolden the charming, dizzy white rabbit. Dot, who was a middle-aged midget, played tiny Alice when she shrank going down the rabbit hole. Frankie was a lewd, but loving, Mad Hatter. He was fond of Dot who made him laugh. One night Frankie gave a party and tried to force Dot to have a drink. "No," she said, "If I do I'll get tipsy and fall over. Midgets don't drink." Anyway, Dot relented, had a drink and promptly fell face down. Frankie hailed a taxi to take her home.

A few days later, an unspeakable event made us realise how vulnerable Dot was. She met her husband after the show and got on the tube to go home when some thugs attacked them, ripping off her tiny wedding ring and necklace, and stealing what money they had. She returned next day with a badly bruised face, sobbing at the loss of her wedding ring. Generously, Frankie took her, plus hubby, off, to the jewellers, to buy a new one and insisted that she take a taxi home each night.

Having had voice lessons I was now going to TV interviews and musical auditions. Tension and disappointment often ruin confidence when time and again you don't get the part. I auditioned for *Bless the Bride*, which was to tour England for five months, and got a part as one of the six sisters.

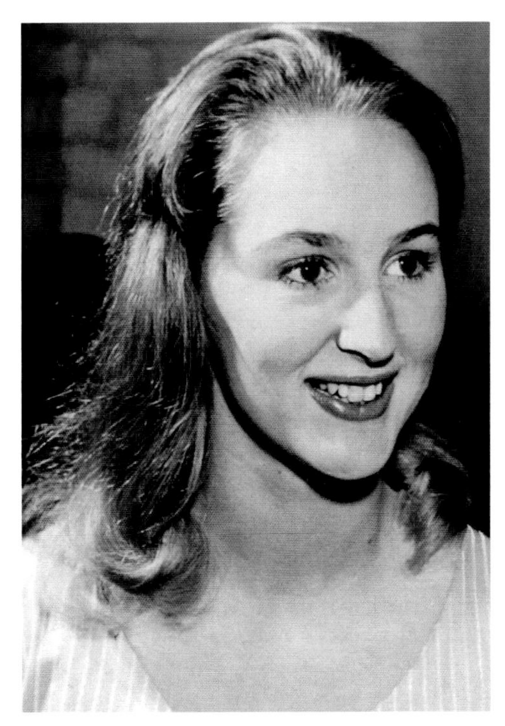

Top left: as Lorinna in Alice in Wonderland; *top right: as a paper doily in* The Snow Goose; *Above:* Bless the Bride *cast, Lotte, 2nd row, centre stage*

Grandpa was thrilled as he had written the songs for this popular, family musical. The Frenchman who played Pierre had a super, handsome body. Whilst in Brighton, when we were sunbathing once on the beach, he suddenly mounted one of the bathing belles and tried to rip off her costume, rather like a panting dog. The dancer was agile enough to jump in the sea and escape.

Touring was an amazing experience, arriving in a strange town on a Sunday when every shop and café was tight shut, which usually meant no supper. The landladies varied. Some were very strict and thought theatricals were wayward and odd. Others were cosy, characterful ladies with many a tale to tell of previous theatre folk. The funniest incident occurred in Newcastle when I brought some shopping home – fish, potatoes, celery and a loofah. I went off to the Empire Theatre and when I returned I found the celery in a vase on the mantelpiece and the loofah awash in white parsley sauce, surrounded by chips looking like floating battleships. The fish had been devoured by the landlady's fat cat.

Touring round the provinces gave me an insight into the different atmosphere in each new venue; the reaction of the audience, the wariness or warmth from the local people. Later I toured in *Belle of New York*, a very old musical, playing Pansy Pins. Just this year as I was taking my daughter and grandson to *Billy Elliott* at the Victoria Palace, going up the stairs I found two posters with my name 'Charlotte Selwyn' billed in the second row. I shrieked with delight.

Right: as Patsy Pinns in
Belle of New York
Below: the poster for the show

Life was interesting living with Granny and Grandpa. Breakfast would be taken in silence as A.P.H. (as Grandpa was known) ploughed through every newspaper, writing down comments and suggestions, usually about politics. Having been the Independent Member for Oxford University and a very individual politician in Parliament, his mind was still razor sharp on many subjects. He also took an interest in my activities and auditions. Some evenings we would sing along together and I would try to hit the high notes to a piece for one of his new musicals.

Both grandparents had an amazing ability to adjust to the new generation's habits and attitudes. During my search for work I met a producer who took an interest in me, rather than my acting. One balmy summer's day he drove me to the country and gently took me in a field on a bed of hay. I felt euphoric and frightened at the same time and had to hide my grandmother's bloodstained skirt when I got home. I told no one of my secret. I thought it would shock them. But I was wrong. About six months later we were having supper, discussing youthful behaviour, when Granny turned to me: "Well, you wouldn't know about it all darling, you're still a virgin, aren't you?"

"Well, actually I'm not," I replied.

"Oh, really? How wonderful! Where did it happen?"

"In a field."

"Oh, happy news, Alan, let's celebrate." So, they got out the champagne as they chortled, "Here's to Charlotte being deflowered." Such an amazing reaction from two Victorian, 60 to 70-year-olds.

Granny taught me to drive. I failed my first test. The solemn instructor said, "Now, Miss Pudney, do an emergency stop on this hill." I put my foot on the accelerator instead of the brake. The car shot forward and my fork struck his neck from the back seat. I had brought my tin cup and cutlery ready for work at a Christmas Post Office job. He looked shocked and angry as we drove back to the base in silence.

Granny was a brilliant chess player and went to many tournaments. One of her friends who came to the house every week was Freddie, a ruddy-faced director of Richmond Theatre. He later auditioned and cast me as the witch in *The Sleeping Beauty* pantomime. I loved it. Whenever I came on stage I got loud boos. I had a pair of rubber gloves with long talons painted on the end, blacked-out teeth and a hag's costume. I had to say one rhyming couplet beside the spinning wheel as I applied poison to it:

'And now this should do the trick,
She'll only feel a tiny prick.'

The cast backstage always chuckled at this point as did the audience. In my naivety I had no idea of the double meaning of 'prick' – until the star of the show whispered in my ear, "You naughty girl," and explained.

Every night I had to crawl into a harness backstage and fly on my broomstick across the stage, cackling loudly. When my mother came one evening, she said, "Oh, do fly across twice Charlotte, I can't wait to see you." Well, Burt who had to pull the ropes up on the pulley was in a muddle. I flew across once and got entwined in the velvet curtains. Burt had to keep me up there in order to unravel broomstick and body and then make a return flight. I saw his eyes popping out of his head as my underwear loosened and hung on the end of the broomstick, by which time he'd left me suspended centre-stage. Then Burt let go! I fell in a heap onto the darkened floor, unhurt, and crawled off while everyone laughed and booed, including my mother.

The next day I received a severe telling-off from the producer. I only ever flew once after that. The next week London Transport had hired the theatre for all their employees and as I sidled on stage was met by a barrage of fruit, eggs and booing. It was a shock, but apparently the L.T. had a penchant for panto baddies.

The annual Boat Race was held on a grand scale in Hammersmith Terrace. Field Marshall Montgomery, Harold Macmillan, Sir Malcolm Sargent and various hand-picked politicians would be swept up to the top room where Grandpa held a select drinks party. Everyone cheered out of the window as the Oxford and Cambridge teams rowed by. Many artists, musicians, as well as family members, came too. I nearly fainted with delight when Margot Fonteyn came one year and I was introduced to this goddess of ballet. Granny was a warm and gracious hostess. She had amazing poise, not to mention immense patience.

I bought a Yorkshire terrier with me, called Mino, when I moved into Number 12. Unfortunately, the dog thought the 50-year-old dusty curtains were trees and kept cocking his leg to pee. "Take the puppy for a walk, Alan," Granny would say. The sight of Grandpa being pulled along The Mall by a playful puppy was unique.

A year later I acquired a pretty hamster called Henrietta. She vanished a week later. After a few days I heard a scrabbling in my bed. Inside the mattress was Henrietta making a nest.

Granny somehow put up with the livestock. She had a great sense of humour too, but her patience was sorely tested every evening when her husband would trundle off to his local, The Black Lion. He would sit in his special corner, sipping pink gins, surrounded by a clutch of regulars and varied professionals, wayfarers, navigators, stokers and numerous young ladies who would sit up close to his twinkling eye. He loved to flirt, even in old age, and was the most wonderful raconteur of unusual stories and jokes, entertaining everyone in the pub. Meanwhile, at home, Granny would have had her second gin and vermouth, prepared supper and be seething as the potatoes grew cold. Grandpa rolled in later than late, oblivious to time or culinary worries.

He had a loyal secretary called Priscilla who spent every day typing letters to Parliament or *The Times*. Often, he would dictate in the sunny garden, wearing very baggy shorts. Priscilla would tap-tap away while Grandpa's favourite terrapins waddled out of the pond and nibbled his toes until he stopped work to feed them Kit-e-Kat.

I shall never forget a large, packed pleasure steamer going by on a high tide and the loudspeaker announcing, "And there on the starboard side is the house where Edgar Alan Poe lived. He was a writer, but he's long dead!"

Grandpa was furious, got up (shorts almost round his ankles), and shouted across the water, "I am Alan Herbert, very much alive and not dead yet!" The steamer hooted and Grandpa later received a letter of apology from the skipper.

Granny and Grandpa often went to stay with the Astors, either at Hever Castle in Kent or in their wonderful villa near Grasse in France. Meanwhile I would house-sit in Hammersmith and occasionally throw the odd, exciting riverside party, with well-known actors remaining in various beds till dawn.

Left: A.P.H. and Granny at 12, Hammersmith Terrace
Below left: 'Winter, Hammersmith Terrace', a watercolour by Brian Lemesle Adams
Below right: in the snow, December 1967

One year Granny asked Lord Astor if she could bring her eldest granddaughter to Hever. It was an alarming experience to be faced with the etiquette of such an aristocratic household. I was shown to my bedroom by the butler. Granny and Grandpa had a suite downstairs overlooking the swimming pool. As I descended the stairs for breakfast two yapping Scottie dogs bit my ankles, so I mounted the banister and slid down to avoid them, only to arrive in front of Lord Astor.

As I entered the breakfast room there were nine covered dishes on the hot plate. The waiter asked what I'd like. I began lifting the hot lids. Granny rescued me by saying, "Try the kedgeree, darling," which I did. Lord Astor slurped his food into a flaccid mouth, his false teeth chewing away.

At Hever from left: A.P.H., Lotte, Lord Astor, Granny, Lady Astor (out of shot)

He and Granny went off with their easels to paint in the beautiful orchard. Later in the morning we were summoned to the swimming pool. Granny had told me on no account to go in the water before Lord Astor. I looked aghast as the eminent Lord unscrewed his left knee, placed half a leg on the side of the pool and started swimming. I certainly swam very delicately that day.

One morning Granny said that John (Lord Astor) wanted to paint me and I was directed upstairs where this drooling old man sat me on his knee and tried to kiss me, then offered me some jewellery and eventually started painting me (with my clothes on, although he would have preferred to have done a nude).

At dinner there was so much cutlery for so many courses. It seemed like a game of chance to see which implement Granny picked up. As for knowing how to eat an artichoke with your hands – I left the heart on my side plate. Granny mouthed, "Eat it." I stuffed it in my mouth whole and then later plucked it out and hid it in my napkin under the table. My handbag contained a few forlorn leftovers which I later flushed down the loo. It was with much relief that I left to meet Arnold Wesker and Bob Swash in Brussels for the opening of Arnold's play, *Their Very Own and Golden City.*

I had become great friends with Arnold and his wife Dusty. In 1961 I had been in his highly successful *The Kitchen* that John Dexter directed; a fantastic, fast-moving production at the Royal Court, with Robert Stephens in the lead. I was terrified of Dexter. He had a sharp tongue and could be very cruel if you didn't keep up with the pace of his production. My aunt, Jocelyn Herbert, had designed the set. The atmosphere created by Jocelyn's pretend, heated oven (made from cardboard boxes) which gave a 'whoosh' as it was ignited, combined with the lightning fast service, made an electrifying climax. Every night the audience rose to their feet at the finale. After the show some of the audience would queue at the stage door, asking for some leftover food – although it was all mimed.

Backstage I had renewed my special friendship with Lynn Redgrave who was helping with the stage management. We used to go back to her parents' flat in Knightsbridge and talk for hours. Lynn's mother, Rachel Kempson, serene as ever, always welcomed me. Later Deirdre, Corin Redgrave's wife, made me godmother to their daughter Gemma. Lynn has, of course, excelled herself in a brilliant acting career, creating many wonderful performances. We remain great friends and I never see enough of her as she lives in the USA.

Vanessa went on to become one of our finest actresses, a unique creature, with a crazy streak of defiance – and oh, that wonderful voice. Her face and smile reflect a special Redgrave beauty.

Years later I used to visit Rachel and listen to her many reminiscences. A remarkable woman of poise and dignity, saying: "Well, I liked Ralph Richardson when he was in so and so. No, I didn't like Larry doing it..." or "Dear John (Gielgud), such a unique voice and timing. I loved working with them all – and Michael too!" I grew very close to Rachel, we laughed often and I miss her dearly.

I also assisted Arnold directing *The Four Seasons* with Alan Bates and Diane Cilento, a very emotive two-hander play. During this time I became involved in The Round House, a vast Victorian engine shed near Chalk Farm. Arnold was desperately trying to raise funds to develop the magnificent building into an arts centre. I was swept up with the idea of creating a small meeting place for poets, so founded a Poetry Theatre in the Annexe and ran it with keen volunteers. We did everything ourselves – chairs, platform and décor – there being virtually no money available. The Liverpool Poets, Brian Patten and Roger McGough gave readings there, as did my father John Pudney.

During this period in the early 1960s I met many directors and producers; Peter Brook, Terry Hands and Herbert Wise to name only three. Irving Wardle, *The Times'* theatre critic, was also an admirer of what I was trying to do. The Round House roared with psychedelic shows starring The Who, The Beatles and Pete Seeger. Even Harold Wilson held a conference there.

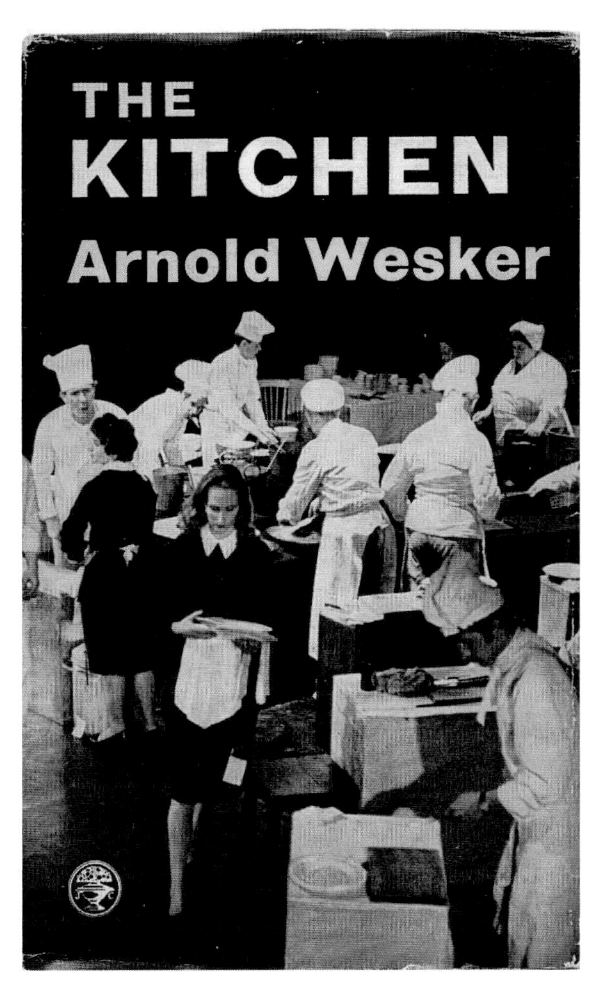

As a waitress, pictured on the dustjacket to The Kitchen *by Arnold Wesker*

The Affair

You are a man, I a woman
We cycle across each other
Encounter the rim of our silent universe.
We touch, we feel – fall down in case we intrude
Eat drink love, all the normal bloody things
But if we truly love – suspect rises up – love is not allowed
We are alive but – but – but –
What does it mean anymore
Let's save each other anyway we can.

Scene 4

From Stage to Screen 1962-1969

In 1962 I auditioned for Bernard Miles' production of a strange play called *The Bedbug* by Mayakovsky, with Joss Ackland playing the lead. Bernard Miles, a larger-than-life character who created the open stage Mermaid Theatre in Puddle Dock on the Thames at Blackfriars, acted in and directed many unusual productions. It was a vibrant, exciting place to work at this time. In the cast was an actor called Tony Beckley. We met after the first rehearsal, as though drawn by an invisible magnetic force. We sat on a bench and talked for five hours. It was the most extraordinary moment of my life. He was to influence profoundly my artistic and emotional life.

Two years later I went to audition for Peter Brook (*Lord of the Flies, The Mahabharata*) who was producing *Marat/Sade* by Peter Weiss for the RSC. He was a very *avant garde* producer and put on a fantastic *A Midsummer Night's Dream.* He asked us to do some weird and sensual writhing on the floor – all improvisation I suppose – to see how we'd interpret madness in the Marat asylum. After the audition I met Johnny Steiner, a lanky, attractive actor, who got a good part in the production opposite Glenda Jackson. We went for a chatty coffee and over the next few months fell in love. It was a very intense, passionate, erotic relationship. About a year later someone began to intrude.

In the middle of the night Johnny got various phone calls. When I asked him who it was, he shrugged his shoulders: "Oh, no one you know." Eventually he revealed *his* (not her) identity: John Schlesinger, the well-known film director had fallen in love with Johnny too. Johnny had never been homosexual and was a very manly, sensual and loving partner. He went round to see John one night, leaving me to sleep on in bed. I left next morning wondering sadly when I'd next see Johnny. He was obviously flattered by the attentions of a famous film director, but was also in conflict about our own special relationship. I found it odd to hear the phone ring in the middle of the night, after Johnny and I had just finished passionate love-making, and see him dress and go over to Schlesinger's house.

A year later John Schlesinger (*Midnight Cowboy, Far From the Madding Crowd*) started casting for a film called *Darling* with Julie Christie and Dirk Bogarde. He asked Johnny to audition for a part and I also got to play a character with him. Schlesinger was intrigued to see us both on camera. I was a little embarrassed, if not bemused, to meet the man who was sharing my lover. He was a kind, amusing and fascinating director. The film was a great success and seeing our relationships interpreted on screen was poignant indeed. Our relationship was very intense by now and he found it too much. Johnny went off to New York for a job. We had one last passionate weekend in a lovely Brighton hotel. He made promises to return - but it never happened. The film *Sunday Bloody Sunday* is our story.

A month later I found I was pregnant. Living with my grandparents, while suffering from morning sickness, was very sad and difficult. I wrote to Johnny who said obviously I must have an abortion - and sent me £300 in cash. A friend found a clinic in Ealing. It wouldn't take cheques. It was all very secret, as abortion was considered shameful and bad in those days. At about two months pregnant I walked through the white clinic doors, terrified and alone, and was shown upstairs to a twin room which was already occupied by a very young, precocious, ginger-haired girl. I was trembling with fear and felt so lonely. Must I do this? I'd always wanted a son – what if this is my son inside me? I had no choice. Circumstances had determined the choice.

"How far gone are you?" asked the girl.

"Oh," I stuttered, "about six weeks."

"I've got twins to get rid of," she said, almost with pride. I was aghast at her blatancy. Her mother said to me, "Never mind, it will soon be over."

Well it was. I felt a raging emptiness and rather sore. The doctor came round a few hours later and said, "All went well. It was a boy. You'll be well enough to go home tomorrow as long as you rest. We need the bed for the next patient." I felt stunned and wept at the loss and the hollowness. What a grotesque, secret business it was then.

I could not go home to my grandparents looking ill and very emotional at my loss. They would have been shocked. Dusty and Arnold Wesker gave me the comfort of their spare room where I gradually came to my senses, surrounded by the bubbly fun of their young children. The dreadful emotional and physical impact on me took months to heal.

I made a few episodes on TV of *Emergency Ward 10* and then two *Saint* stories. We were filming a Roger Moore sequence in a car chase on location in Hertfordshire. I shan't forget an elongated make-up session (prior to this shot) where Roger demanded every single hair be combed and shaped towards the side, primped down with some sort of gel. We watched in amazement at the preening he insisted on before each take. Sitting in the polished, open limousine, he started to drive when a gust of wind caught his hair, turning it into a mop. He was furious and we all waited again while the hair was smoothed down. He was a very vain man.

During another sequence a group of girls and chaps were standing in the back of the jeep. As the vehicle came to an abrupt half we girls were meant to jump down into the arms of our male partner. Alas, when I jumped no one caught me and I tore all the muscles in my ankle. After A&E I spent several weeks on crutches, followed by several months trying to get compensation out of the film company. After a long, legal battle I finally received some small amount for injury and loss of work.

Mondays

Heavy – the senseless shriek has begun again
Heavy – the dull awakening to yet another Monday, a week the same
Perpetual tasks, fruitless efforts, drab sights, crude, violent sounds
Daily sounds of neither sense nor sensitivity wrenching the membranes from a delicate ear
The most beautiful entry to our brain – that tormented battery
Battered to numb confusion. Some days it just limps aimlessly
In surrender to the battles of pressure and pain and the surging futility.

Fatigued limbs crawl into expectant garments, force the feet into motion
Pushing past equally stale faces suffering the relapse of the flabby Sunday
Previously spent indolently caged in a heap or purging the system with sudden exercise
Monday a false premise of innocently assembled plans, still shuffling later,
OK being shunted on (when Friday comes) to yet another forfeit – Monday again
Carpets ploughed, washing pumped, remnants churned from the weekend gorging
Refuse groaning into raucous pulp, stale produce yawns while quantity is rearranged
Time mocking – whips round the hat and glimpses at the clouds for mood.
Reluctant (habits near) thought swerves to avoid the pattern of heaviness
So insistent is one tame task, it lays traps for all the rest.
The week has opened up its store with less and less to sell for me anymore
Heaviness, apprehension, an overwhelming sadness
I slide back to my senses and gently lock them away
Monday again...

Working on several episodes of *The Avengers* series I was fascinated by Honor Blackman. Honor was quite brusque and wore a tough outer shell, whilst playing some ruthless characters dressed in black leather. Yet she had a sensuality and a mocking laugh which covered a lot of personal problems. There was a scene in a prison cell where I had to help a prisoner escape by dropping a key into her tin mug of coffee so she could unlock the cell door that night.

Several takes later, after the key had first caught the mug and fallen to the floor, then sunk to the bottom of the mug, splashing me and the camera, the shot was over and Honor Blackman said, laughingly, "That took some time. I'd have had breakfast if I'd known." I still receive miniscule cheques for repeats of *The Avengers*.

In one of the various TV shows I was in, I played a waitress with a fairly short flowery skirt. While waiting for the next scene I was suddenly goosed from behind. I turned to see a grinning Tony Booth, the actor and father of Cherie Blair - but I didn't find it funny.

I had moved into a first-floor bedsit just up the road from Granny. The landlady was called Mrs Spittle, an ancient eccentric. Her kitchen had been cut in half to accommodate a bath which was partitioned off and only to be used once a week for a few bob - and *then* with just three inches of water. The toilet was outside, under a corrugated roof. No peeing after 10pm – so we were given a pot for the night. On Friday nights she cooked tripe and onions. The smell was revolting and I tried to have supper elsewhere on Fridays. Living in a bedsit I used to feel ferociously lonely and had bouts of utter depression, almost suicidal. The world seemed too big for me to be a part of. I felt a stranger to its unity. I could barely cope with the struggles within my soul.

Eventually I realised that it was essential for an actress to have a phone. Mrs Spittle was terrified of them and had never dared use one. After several months my grandmother persuaded her it was vital for my work and she consented. One night there was a knock on my bed-sit door. "Would you use that machine to call my friend please?" Her hands were trembling as she handed me some money.

There was a strict rule that visitors were out by 10pm. This had become impossible when Johnny Steiner had visited me for what turned out to be a hushed night of great passion on a loosely strung, squashy bed. Sometimes she banged on the ceiling with her stick, shouting, "What are you doing?"

I would reply: "My exercises for acting and breathing!" Poor Johnny used to make some hair-raising escapes. I would have to go downstairs hoping that Mrs Spittle was in the kitchen, and leave the front door open for him. I'd keep her talking while Johnny crept out. Once she caught him at the front door. He'd got his cap on and pretended he wanted to read her meter. One morning he climbed down the drainpipe, thinking she was in the loo, but she was talking to a neighbour up the alley, where we'd just emptied the full pee pot out of the window.

In reflective mood

Afterwards

What's left? The potency of a cigar lingering in the room
The tang upon my lips and in between my legs,
But that will go – as they went – hurriedly once over.
A gull stands resolute upon a chimney pot
I admire his determination.
The river lilts by to empty her banks of refuse left on the flood tide.
People go home wildly to their machines,
I put on music and am silent and want silence.
Someone came and activated a natural instinct, but I felt debased strongly.
My limbs need no play-time, my veins need a pulse to warm them as the rivers flow.
Yes, I felt, I gave, and mistimed, sighed without my guest awaiting the signal.
Union of bodies or of minds is terribly important in this scared age of defiance.
I clear up the ash, ache a lot, yet cannot sleep; I am not fulfilled.
I tidy the bed – I know it will happen again and repeat the same insufficiency.
I put on more music and don't carry myself happily.

Thank goodness when I later moved into my own flat above the local corner shop, there were no rules about male visitors. I had to get tenants to help with the rent. I lived very frugally, surviving on two pieces of bacon a week, and often poaching supper from Granny.

A series of very complex men rented the room from me, among them John Antrobus, Spike Milligan and a weird writer who never seemed to wake up.

I never had girls as tenants because of their endless washing. Most of these chaps never washed, threw their socks away or had very few clothes, and were often out. Once there was a murky visit from a middle-aged man who sailed a lot. He brought some potato cakes to fry. Innocently I ate two. My God, they were hash cakes! My head exploded and thundered, I became almost delirious and collapsed on the bed, feeling wretched. He left laughing. I never saw him again.

Many well-known directors, actors, film assistants and writers came to various wild parties in this flat. Heaps of bodies slept off the fun, lying on the stairs or in the empty bath. Not quite orgies, I invited a weird and wonderful mix of the famous, the kinky and the gay to these parties, who I had previously entertained at Granny's house by the Thames when she went away on holiday.

There I'd go upstairs and find John Hurt green with alcohol and with a girlfriend he didn't want. Other revellers included David Mercer, Nigel Williamson, Jeremy Brett, John Fraser, Peter Brook and lots of Royal Court actors. 'Spliff circles' formed as Biba and the Beatles began to hit the headlines.

In 1967 I was in Roman Polanski's *Dance of the Vampires*, mentioned earlier. His wife Sharon Tate was also in the film, before she was brutally murdered by a vicious cult a few years later. He was a fascinating man to work with and a perfectionist.

The whole set was built among the Hertfordshire fields which had to be covered in artificial snow, and every indoor set adorned with massive bulbs of real garlic (swinging around like ogres' balls). The sleigh and reindeer bringing the vampire's hosts ploughed through the hot ice on a boiling day in the high '70s, while the thick snow melted. The whole film was a send-up and such fun to work on.

Having had the pleasure of working in several TV productions with dear Charles Jarrott (*Condorman, Mary Queen of Scots*), he later cast me in his superb film *Anne of the Thousand Days*. I played lady-in-waiting to Anne Boleyn. Richard Burton was a robust Henry VIII to gentle Genevieve Bujold's Anne. Huge roaring log fires and enormous Great Danes adorned one set, while outside hundreds of extras performed in thick, heavy Tudor costumes. Various over-heated ladies keeled over, fainting in the heat of a summer's day. The vast crowd impassively watched them carried off and replaced.

Burton behaved very high-handedly. If he felt like a couple of days' holiday in Wales he'd go – leaving great disruption behind him, letting everyone down. He would wink at a pretty girl, demanding she "come hither for him to toy with," in his dressing room. When we arrived at 6am for our make-up calls, we could hear Burton making strange noises in his dressing room, but forgave him for his roguishness since that voice of his and his acting were incredible. I was livid when the few lines I had in a chapel scene were taken by Liz Taylor who fancied the role for herself. A special dress, similar to my beautiful one, was made for her and I was deprived of a very appealing cameo part.

The execution scene was harrowing indeed. A large platform was erected in a big square with the entire crowd peering as a petite Anne was escorted to the scaffold. All the ladies-in-waiting were given little pessaries to put up their noses to bring on tears, because we couldn't cry to order during the three hours' shooting. When the axe came down there was a deathly silence which Charles had engendered with his powerful, yet sensitive, direction.

During this happy location work I met Amanda Walker, another lady-in-waiting, who has become one of my closest friends. We've shared much laughter and sadness over the years. She greatly understood my profound sensitivity and has helped so much with all the pain I've been through.

She and her husband, the wonderful actor Patrick Godfrey, nicknamed me Willow, like the tree swaying and yielding to the sun.

It was most interesting to watch a lot of famous faces acting inside their remarkable Tudor costumes; while Richard's extraordinarily powerful voice rang through us all. Genevieve gave a most touching performance as Anne Boleyn, her tiny neck so vulnerable to the axe. I met Chris at this time and brought him to see the rehearsals. He was astonished at the realistic sets.

As lady-in-waiting in Anne of the Thousand Days

Ice White

The peppery blizzard iced the city
Pearl-grey mist blanketed the horizon
Muffled engines tip-toed the chaotic highway.
Busy streets emptied into a serene hushed silence
Branches stretched sparkling enmeshed in a fretwork
Of iced diamonds – windows and people hooded in snow-capped clusters.

Breath freezing in the beauty and stillness of the white night
Next morning frost filigree hugged window panes
Hot white sun pierced the black iced roads
And gulls lined the river bed like a coral necklace in sun startled light.

Roof tiles begin to melt – dribbling across the yawning houses
A tranquil day caught the frost and humbled the world
To soften the pace and turn in towards the quilted warmth of home.

Scene 5

Family 1969-2007

In 1964 dear Granny and Grandpa were given a surprise Golden Wedding party at their daughter Jocelyn and George Devine's flat in Chelsea. Grandpa had commissioned the jewellers to design 50 sovereigns into a lovely necklace. It was such a happy party. I was washing up and clearing away afterwards till dawn. Twenty years later Granny's birthday was celebrated at home by the river, and many of her great friends came, including Sir Gerald Fitzmaurice, a very eminent lawyer who was head of the Hague Law Courts.

He was a secret admirer of Granny and used to send her huge parcels of recently published books. On her birthday or anniversary he'd take her to concerts or on special, grand dinner dates. He adored her, and she liked and was flattered by his attentions. His wife Lady Evelina was a marvellous, eccentric lady to whom I grew very close. She had the wildest sense of humour. Though aware of her husband's position she could turn a posh or grand 'do' into a hilarious event. She had one poor son James who stuttered terribly and was a bit simple. Alas, he fell in love with me, but I never understood a word he said because of his awful speech impediment. He died young.

Granny's 80th birthday party was in full swing and Uncle John was at the piano, playing *This is My Lovely Day* and *God Bless the Family*, when Sir Gerald, always scarlet in the face, entered the drawing room, then quietly and promptly fell down dead by the door. Granny was shielded in her chair by various relatives, while John, also oblivious, continued to play.

Our local doctor, one of the guests, pronounced him dead and rang for an ambulance. Meanwhile, no one could get out of the room as he lay across the entrance. The ambulance refused to come unless he was alive - due to a strike - so he was carried to a car. The guests, mostly unaware, were told that supper would be served next door at Uncle John's house. No one could bear to tell Granny her best friend had passed away at her birthday party. Later, she sadly read in the press he'd died (though not where it had happened) and missed him greatly.

Years before, another of Granny's friends, artist Raymond Coxon, my godfather, asked me to model for him at his Chelsea art classes. One week I posed nude and was shocked after three hours to find that some had painted my pubes green, my pert, small breasts a blue hue and my slim body a sort of pale orange. All the artists discussed their own version of me.

I was encouraged to return the following week when I spent another three hours (numbly) with my back to the class. Some very flattering curves and, again, strange colourful visions emerged; everyone portrayed me differently. Raymond was a blunt Lancashire man with a stabbing sense of humour.

I also modelled for Pandora Astor in her sumptuous house in Chelsea. She was young, very rich and quite gentle. She loved my willowy torso and painted me in the nude and in various pieces of underclothes, using oils and pastels, but would hurriedly put all the artists' materials away when she heard her husband, Michael, return home. She paid me generously which helped with the rent.

Having often suffered weeks and months out of work – like everyone in the acting profession – I earned money looking after children of all ages. I was able to give them affection and love, and their fun filled a growing yearning to have children myself and get married. I was in my thirties and most relationships failed because I so desperately wanted them to work and gave too much (which sometimes overwhelmed the cautious man).

Finally, fate gave me a much-needed reward - a new life. While out of work I looked after Chris Moore's children, Andy and Sarah, aged two and four, whose mother, Sue, was going out with Lord Thynne and, after a very acrimonious divorce, left. In time I gradually fell in love with this dear, special, but tortured man, and a year later we married – alas, in a register office in Hammersmith. I'd dreamt of a white wedding since I was six and used to dress up my cats for a feline version with the kittens as bridesmaids. The toad played the vicar.

Giving up my career, I decided to devote myself one hundred percent to my step-children and my new husband. Becoming a step-mother was a thankless role. No matter how much I loved and cared for Andy and Sarah their mother tried to turn them against me. Also, I was longing for children of our own. Our firstborn was Zoë, who we thought would be a boy because she kicked inside me so much.

Chris took me to the Sistine Chapel in Rome when I was six months' pregnant (on a belated honeymoon) and pronounced the babe should be Zacharias, but 'she' shot out of me at great speed and has never stopped running since. The name Zoë means 'life' in Greek.

An agonising, ectopic pregnancy followed three years later. I was very ill and lost one fallopian tube. A year later, I lost a much-wanted son, Joe, who lived for only 12 hours.

Finally, after a great struggle, we produced Daisy, a very beautiful girl. Gazing at her I said to the nurse, "She's going to be a cellist". Seven years later she started to play and gave us many wonderful musical years, with the piano too. Since becoming a nurse she has no time, alas, for the bow or keyboard. She tied the knot in 2005 with a newly qualified doctor, Rob Horsley, and they've moved to York. They've just produced Will who came to London in 2006 to be baby Jesus in my annual Nativity play.

Good Morning

Good morning –
How are you?
I cherish you –
Want you –
Come soon
Touch me again
Where – when – no why, no how
Just now
Peace – Hello
I'm here.

Chris in fancy dress in Corfu

Above: Zoë; below: Daisy
Top right: Mum and her chicks
Right: as bridesmaids
Bottom right: as acolyte and boat girl at St Nicholas Church

Above: Zoë, Lotte, Chris and Daisy
Below left: Chris's speech at Daisy and Rob's wedding; below right: Imi, Daisy's bridesmaid and Lotte

Zoë has a delicious son Daniel, aged 10, who I love dearly and is currently at school here in England. Whenever he comes to London I take him to the Lyric or other theatres. He's captivated by live performance. After seeing *The Snowman*, aged four, he stood up in the stalls and called to the stage, "It's great! Could you do it again, NOW!" He has a little sister called Mimi and is so generous-spirited, showing no envy of the attention she receives; indeed he is protective of her. She has often enjoyed my music classes and is a gifted, musical, happy child, aged three. Alas, I don't see her much as she lives in Corfu with her mother and Francis, and I wish Mimi was here more often so I could get to know her better.

My parents always chided me that I was the oldest, yet still unmarried. All my siblings and step-siblings got married to great cheer, but my life turned around in 1971 when I married Chris. We're now celebrating 35 years together! With my own brother and sister divorced I feel it a great achievement to have stayed the course. Despite being pregnant five times I have only two children. The pain and loss has made me cherish them even more. It's sad, of course, in one's latter years, that both daughters aren't in London and so our contact is intermittent and often rushed.

At my Daisy's wedding I had to buy some mules (because of bunions I couldn't find shoes to match the dress). I decided to stick my shoes to my socks with UHU glue, over which I wore elastic stockings for varicose veins. Halfway through the wedding, I said to Chris, "My feet are desperately escaping my mules". We sat on the steps and he pulled and pulled – the UHU wouldn't budge. Finally, he yanked off mules and socks, and put them in a vase of flowers. I retained my dignity as mother of the bride in stockinged feet...

Thank God I'm not an actress now, because I forget so many obvious things, yet I still teach little ones and put on a wonderful Nativity Play every year at old people's homes in Chiswick and Hammersmith. I order one or two baby Jesus from some mums who have three-month-old babies of either sex (no one knows if it's a boy or a girl). After the interval we sing a variety of nostalgic songs, *Knees up Mother Brown* or *Oh, I Do Like to be Beside the Seaside*. Lots of elderly knees go up and down in the wheel chairs, legs flying out to the tune. It's fantastic to see young and old enjoy the songs together. There's such an explosion of joy – it's worth waiting all the days in the year. The Sister at the convent said, "It's a miracle what your concert has done to the old ladies, they have all started singing in bed!" This year (2006), a 103-year-old lady sat in the front row, singing all the old songs, alongside children four or even five generations younger.

I'm now almost the same age as some of the oldies. If, when I die, I could leave a loving legacy to everyone at Christmas it would be this: wherever you are, organise a Nativity play with a live baby Jesus, fill a hall with old people, and get everyone singing at the end to some old-fashioned, nostalgic songs. What a simple joyous gift that would be for all concerned, from nought to 80.

Nativity Plays

Mimi as Baby Jesus and Dan a King

Dan as Baby Jesus

Singing at the convent

Vignettes

Spring

How suddenly the air is free
As spring bursts forth for us to see.
The first buds out, adorn the parks
And some are set, as lighted sparks
All colours – crocus' crops begin
Sweet daffodils shine out to win
The fragrance best of fellow flowers,
They fight through all those ghastly showers.

People dashing to and fro
Begin to notice and to know
How spring can change the wind again
And make the sun return from Spain.
Thousands swarm like buzzing bees
To London's parks and pubs and trees
They smile – as Nature draws them on
With beauty bles't but never gone.

1. *Gwendolen Herbert, née Quilter*
My Dear Granny

I grew to love and appreciate Granny more than any other relative. She had a very strict upbringing and wasn't even educated. She learned everything through her love of reading. Her mother was Hungarian and her English father, Harry Quilter, travelled as an artist and buyer of pictures.

Her mother took her and sisters Magdalene, Lois and April, along with brothers Ted and Denis, on many gallery visits, holidays in Cornwall, and musical soirées. The Quilter family was very musical. Her husband having died early, Gwendolyn's mother married a tall academic called Frank - who later coached my Aunt Lavender and Uncle John in scholastic work.

Granny became an exceptional concert pianist and studied in Paris. She also began to paint, in particular still-life. Her self-taught knowledge enabled her to read Proust, Balzac, Mauriac and de Maupassant in French, while her sharp intelligence gave her a good understanding of German. She also absorbed and learnt a vast range of poetry.

While playing tennis with friends Granny was attracted by a voice on the adjoining court and caught sight of the accompanying knees. It was A. P. Herbert cavorting and laughing whilst playing. She was smitten instantly by his character. Later they happened to meet at Oxford House in Bethnal Green. The mutual attraction developed into a brief courtship due to the imminence of war. He would meet her in a café and take up a spoon and teach her Morse code on the tumblers. They married on the last day of 1914 at Red Church, Bethnal Green, spent four days on honeymoon in Fulham Road before he left to fight at Gallipoli. She knew little about his family except that they had lived in Machroes Abbey in Tipperary many years before.

Granny was very naïve when she married. She recounted to me how she felt unwell and walked from Hammersmith to Kensington to see her doctor. After an examination he told her she was pregnant and she promptly fainted with shock. He gave her smelling salts.

"Oh, but I only spent two nights with Alan before he went off to Gallipoli," she later said.

My mother Crystal arrived nine months later, born at home. They were shocked not to see a boy. Granny went on to have two more daughters, Jocelyn and Lavender. A few years later John arrived: "He was an accident - I don't know how it happened."

He was born overdue, after Granny had been taken out in a dinghy on a windy day to bring on the contractions. Hence John's love of boats maybe!

Though there were governesses and maids to help Granny run the household, she devoted herself entirely to A.P.H. (as Grandpa was known), taking the children away on holidays to allow the 'Independent Member' to attend to his politics. By nature she was modest and unassuming, yet had a beautiful dignity that shone around her. Her graceful stance and almost lilting walk grew more remarkable in her seventies.

A cheeky sense of humour gave way to such understanding and generosity to others. She lovingly gave me, the eldest of her 16 grandchildren, the ability to believe in myself a little. She also gave me her gifts of generosity and listening. She was rich in so many rare qualities and always seemed to be up with the new generation and attitudes. Little shocked her. She overcame prejudice by her unique ability to discover new areas and then digest it all quietly.

As Granny grew frail in old age, she went to stay with her daughter Lavender. Even then her sense of humour amazed us. She was given special heart pills for angina and took them with her tea in bed. One day when her glasses were missing, we drew the bed back and in our search found dozens of the little pink pills. Granny looked up and gave us her twinkling smile, "You see, I've managed without them," astounding us all. Sadly, dear Gran was suddenly taken ill in great pain with a blockage and went to hospital against her will. She hated being there and even on the operating table struggled to get off. After a major operation she died a few days later, aged 96, on 16 August 1988. I was away in Corfu but paid my loving respect to her in the funeral parlour on my return.

I thank her so much for all the kind encouragement she gave me. She saved my life and gave me a chance. I love her and so wish she was still here. How much Gran would enjoy the fact that I continue to give music classes to small children.

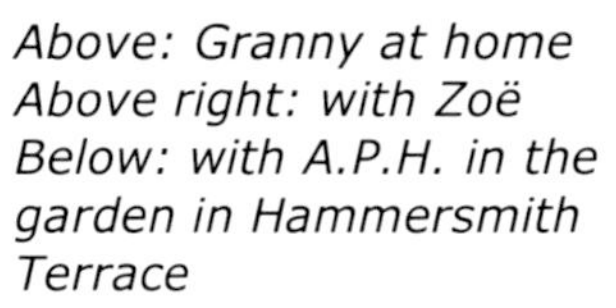

Above: Granny at home
Above right: with Zoë
Below: with A.P.H. in the garden in Hammersmith Terrace

2. A. P. Herbert
Grandpa

Grandpa was the eldest of three sons, Alan, Sidney and Owen. He had a happy childhood and was only beaten a few times for not eating his sago or tapioca pudding. His mother, Beatrice Eugenie Selwyn, daughter of the famous Bishop of New Zealand, married his father, Patrick Herbert, on 7 December 1889. A.P.H. inherited the famous Selwyn family nose.His mother Beatrice died of TB at 33 when he was eight and he was packed off to boarding school. His family life was enhanced by the arrival of Nanny Deakie, a small-framed spinster who became the strongest influence in the Herbert boys' upbringing. At school he learned the piano which was to contribute so much later to his creative musicals.

At Winchester College, his brilliant talent for verse and public speaking won him the King's gold medal award twice. He was also good on the playing fields. His family holidays were always taken at the 'watering places' of Hastings, Brighton or Bournemouth. In London horse-drawn carriages still ruled the roads and he rode a bike wherever possible.

He loved Latin, Greek and English – reading the 21st book of *The Iliad* in preparation for Oxford. He was an enthusiastic classical scholar. His first set of classical verse appeared in *Punch*, August 1910, while still at Winchester.

On leaving New College, Oxford, with a First in jurisprudence, he enlisted as an ordinary seaman in the RNVR, the Royal Naval Division, training at the Crystal Palace. He met Gwen, courted and married her, but found himself at Gallipoli, where he was wounded in the left buttock, but saved by his hip flask of brandy. One brother was killed on the Somme; the other went down with *HMS Hood* in the Second World War.

Instead of being called to the Inner Temple, he decided to write a book about the War called *The Secret Battle*. Sir Winston Churchill later wrote an introduction for it, who thought it one of the best books he had ever read. Working as an MP and for a KC (King's Counsel) he had to write at weekends, starting with *Misleading Cases in the Common Law*. He wrote 80 books in all and contributed to *Punch* weekly.

The Herberts moved from Kensington in 1915 to a rented house, 12, Hammersmith Terrace, and A.P.H. became passionate about the Thames, as well as its watermen and lightermen who manoeuvre the huge lighters up and down the river. He taught his family to sail and eventually acquired *Water Gipsy* which was to play a vital part in the Second World War.

Sometimes Granny and Grandpa held raucous swimming parties, diving off the *Water Gipsy* moored at the end of the garden. I can only suppose the Thames was cleaner then.

The boat race parties were full of great characters; Clement Attlee, Sir Winston Churchill, Charlie Chaplin, Dora Bryan, Dame Margot Fonteyn, Sir Malcolm Sargent, Harold Nicolson and Field Marshall Montgomery.

In 1935 A.P.H. became the Independent Member for Oxford University and instantly introduced a Bill to reform the divorce laws. It was passed in 1937, a great achievement for an Independent Member. He fought for many causes; to banish entertainment tax on books, reform the licensing laws and introduce the Public Lending Right.

The Second World War came. His boat, the *Water Gipsy*, joined the river emergency service, doing many important manoeuvres, and A.P.H. helped teach Morse code and semaphore on some of the steamers which became river ambulances. The *Water Gipsy* was armed with a Lewis gun, rifles, cutlasses in racks about the bunks and hand grenades. The day War was declared, A.P.H. ran out of Parliament to the river bank and jumped aboard, waved off by many MPs. During hostilities they steamed 20,000 miles between Holehaven and Westminster, carrying supplies to barges, and organising a mine watching service and up and down the Thames.

After the War, A.P.H. turned to a totally different occupation, writing musicals with C.B. Cochran and Vivien Ellis. *Bless the Bride* became a resounding success and played in the West End for several years, followed by *Big Ben*, *Tough at the Top*, *Derby Day* and finally *The Water Gypsies*. Grandpa and Vivien would pound away at the piano, composing and altering lyrics and notes with joyous enthusiasm. Ruby was a devoted housekeeper who thought nothing of dusting round a sleeping A.P.H., sprawled across the desk after rehearsing with the 'Cochran Young Ladies' till dawn.

Grandpa had an enormous interest in everyday activities, new laws and people's rights. All news stimulated his interest, and endless letters were written to *The Times* and *Punch* (often detailed and questioning), on many a subject. His wit, as sharp as ever, often stimulated a vigorous argument and he even silenced George Bernard Shaw in one *Times* dispute.

Reading about him now, it humbles me to realise that while living with him and Granny, I never quite appreciated his greatness; how for example, he *never* stopped writing. He had outstanding concentration, being able to write in a crowded pub, on a bus or in a boat.

The tragic end of this remarkable man came as the cruellest blow. In 1970 he had a massive stroke which left him unable to speak. How humiliating for a great man of words and speeches. He was trapped inside himself like a silent prisoner. I remember his eyes appealing to us and the nurses: "Let me go." Oh, the Grandpa I loved and shared some great and funny times with! I was the eldest of his 16 grandchildren and the closest.

Let's stop somebody from doing something!
Everybody does too much.
People seem to think they've a right to eat and drink,
Talk and walk and respirate and rink,
Bicycle and bathe and such.

So let's have lots of little regulations,
Let's make laws and jobs for our relations,
There's too much kissing at the railway stations.
Let's find out what everyone is doing,
And then stop everyone from doing it.

A.P.H.

Lavender and Chris Clarke's wedding day. Lotte (from left), Tessa, A.P.H., cousins Sandra and Jenny

To Grandpa on Your Ending

You wrote a song once called 'God Bless the Family',
I sang it often and was proud of you dear
Abraham, our family's shroud
Can I but weep to see you gone
Your challenge spent, your spirit overrun.
Hot summer's days and music did we share
With terrapins, papers, Granny's chess and hours of care
Too often did you strike a single note
That made me think and nearly choke
But yet we had sweet tender hours
When mad I was to discuss the Indian chars.
Close to you through years of living
Near and with you – so much goes now without your thinking.
In your presence was much learning done
And to people, friends you gave much fun
Yet fighting too, your battles often won
Your peace was not the life but all that was done.

John Pudney

3. John Pudney
My Father

My dad was the only son of a farmer whose land stretched for miles around Slough. Now of course it's covered by the M4 motorway, completely obliterating the rich, arable countryside. His father was a methodical and pedantic man, doing everything at a fixed time.

The arrival of John into a parlour of silent relatives was welcomed with upright detachment, except for his mother – a large-boned, warm woman, who had been a nurse in Australia. Dad loved her and believed all her stories about God doing this and that to us for comfort. He had a very lonely, early childhood with no friends in Langley. Finally, he sneaked out to play with the local village lads, whose language and manners seemed such an adventure compared to his isolated world. There was no television in those days, so he often made up imaginary people to play with or talk to - which is probably why he started writing poetry at an early age.

His mother and father took him to London once to a pantomime. He was so intrigued with the lively, big city he longed to see more of it. At the age of seven he was sent to boarding school, as there were no proper schools nearby. It terrified him; he wet the bed, cried, was sick and missed the empty surroundings back home with his mum indoors.

Eventually he made friends and then moved on to Greshams in Norfolk. The death of his mother during his first year affected him dreadfully. He came home for the funeral to find strange aunts and uncles mumbling to him. His father never hugged him, just looked down and squeezed his hand - and from then on said little to his son. The house felt empty without the warmth of his mother. He found her glove, wrapped it and buried it in the garden.

He didn't do well academically at Greshams, so aged 17 took off to London to become an estate agent trainee. There he finally began to grow up. He began writing articles and became a reporter with the *News Chronicle* and later edited *The Listener*. He had his first novel published and gained recognition for his work from contemporaries like W.H. Auden, Arnold Bennett, Dylan Thomas and W.B. Yates.

At this time Dad met an inspiring, eccentric man called Nelson Illingworth, a crazy Australian journalist living with Kay Murphy (who later became my godmother). They had an attic flat in Regent Street and Kay was the head of Linguaphone, the language school. She often gave me good advice, appreciating the family problems. They both adored Dad and I often stayed at their bungalow on the Thames near Staines. It was like a holiday and Nelson sometimes put me in his little dinghy with a plate of lettuce, a bottle of salad cream (which I loved) and cast off the mooring, saying, "Go on girl, get rowing!" I was petrified at first, but what confidence it gave me when I finally got the oars sorted out. How we laughed.

Dad, having been a very shy, late developer, both physically and socially, found that London helped him experience sex, flirting, drinking, even laughing and finally, love. Marrying Crystal Herbert in 1935, eldest daughter of A.P. Herbert, they produced me a year later, named after Charlotte Street in Soho, where they used to live.

Dad worked for the BBC on many diverse programmes at this time and the family moved to an Essex farmhouse, A much-wanted son and heir, Jeremy, was born and Mum, an intelligent and liberated female, was contributing to journals and translating books. Then the War came, Dad joined the RAF Intelligence Corps and I was sent to safety to a Herefordshire boarding school which I have talked about elsewhere.

After the War and now living in Kent, I remember Dad making us all do funny stunts after lunch, getting up on a chair, reciting a poem or becoming a talking onion. He encouraged us to grow vegetables but he became increasingly cooped up in his office, writing. Mum gave many parties for well-known writers and politicians, and Dad took up politics, standing for the Labour Party; but their relationship began to go wrong and rows started.

Much later Dad came to ballet school and wept, saying he was divorcing Crystal, who was having an affair with Lionel Hale, the broadcaster and writer. Those were such sad and painful times, for him and me.

He was disappointed when I went to ballet school, thinking it a waste of time. Even when I got into the Royal Opera Ballet he still thought I should study something else. Then I started acting and he gave up on me ever having a decent, reliable job. Finally, when I married and gave myself to looking after Chris's children, he began to admire and appreciate all I was capable of. So, ironically, I became closer to him, I hadn't let him down in the end. In his 60s my father became involved with new poets and artists. His appetite for new ideas introduced him to many new friends, including Gavin Henderson, Tim Gordon and Joe Holden. Gavin's Baroque Brass Ensemble played very movingly at his funeral.

Although his eldest child, I was the last to marry. Dad was very fond of Chris - an honest, devoted father who showed great interest in Dad's writings. Not realising that he was about to be overrun by cancer Dad embarked on his last work. Arduous filming started in Egypt for a film he'd written about Thomas Cook. He often related a hilarious event when riding a camel which bolted with him into the desert. It took some hours for the cameramen and guides to find and bring him back. In a banquet scene, although his unknown cancer was constricting his speech, he had to eat gargantuan meals on set. Then he began to lose his voice as the agonising throat cancer began to take hold, gradually taking away his dignity. Returning home, Monica his wife, had to feed him through a pipe into his stomach. She was a devoted carer and cherished him tenderly.

Dad had gone - there was nothing left of him now - a silent shadow imprisoned in a silent body - what a way to go. The affection I missed as a child grew in his last years, late but most welcome. Dad's awful slow death left me longing for him to have seen my own children grown into happy childhood.

Dad wrote about 60 books. Novels, children's stories, lots of poetry, biographies of figures including subjects such as Isambard Brunel, Charles Wesley, Thomas Cook, Lewis Carroll and tomes on the Age of Steam and London Docks. He was interested in so many aspects of life. Even the *Cutty Sark*, near where he lived in latter years, had John Pudney's poetry read on her decks.

Papa

In my file are lots of beauties
Frail or funny, strident songs.
The poet's day is full of duties
Loving you where your pride belongs.
Fate has dealt a cruel card
Silencing you in your own backyard.

In my file it's lots of you
Yours that glow and shout at us
Poems peel into knowledge anew
Ringing in truth with so little fuss
Silence has a powerful strength
Loving has the longest length.

Mother

Have you ever looked at her and wondered who she was?
Or looked in disbelief of your arrival that had no response.
Perhaps you're a mistake that compromised all she didn't like
And thrust out of anticipation came your unrewarding plight.
We all need her from time to time, to know us well and tell us so
There is no substitute for her if there she is to welcome our woe.
We want her to share in our success, to understand our failure,
Take interest in our progress, guide, advise, but nourish the insecure
Moving in directions alien to her own. Does she never wonder where we roam?
Or if you love or lack too much, yet to arrive, to never know home.
What's she really like, is she really her? Why am I so far from what put me here?
Time treads across my face, the pain forgives a sometime tear.

4. *Crystal Herbert*
My Mother

I discovered my mother's final, damaging act after she died. Her will shattered me to depths I'd never known before. I was the eldest of her three children with my father. She also had a daughter by her second marriage and a step-son and step-daughter. She divided her estate first to my younger sister Tessa, second to my half-sister Becca and then to my brother Jeremy, leaving me at the bottom with the least money. It bore out her hurtful attitude towards her first-born. The pain was immeasurable. Also, of course, I could no longer ask her why she disliked me so. She was gone.

As a small child, I began to feel rejected when my much-loved brother Jeremy arrived. At boarding school in Herefordshire, aged five, I felt homesick and a deep insecurity grew inside me. My sister, five years later, was born at home. We could hear nurses' voices and my mother howling away. Tessa was much adored straight away.

My mother was extremely domineering. It grew worse as she got older. She became impatient with my extreme sensitivity. I hardly remember getting praise for anything. Her destructiveness seeped into my young soul, crushing my confidence. Her dislike bewildered me when I needed love and affection. I loved the smell of her knees while sitting on the floor. I noticed her affection especially for Tessa, and also for Jeremy. They got used to me always being told off for this or that.

We were often smacked for being rude, sometimes with a hairbrush. Once, it broke on me, how I laughed. Perhaps I deserved it, I cannot remember the reason.

Mum and Dad both had healthy tempers. Later at my ballet school, Mum would ring up during classes, giving orders: "Do this or that, are you listening, Charlotte?" It went on for hours - so I hung the phone on the banisters during class and each girl would take up the phone and say, "Yes Mum," while she ranted on. Finally the class finished. "Now have you remembered all I said?" she asked. "Yes," I lied.

I hated the way she dominated Dad and how she put on an act whenever visitors came - especially the famous ones.

When the rows started with Dad, I could hear yelling and things being thrown across the room. But Mum's deceit was the worst. When she began an affair with Lionel Hale in London, Dad would be out in the garden while she was on the phone, cooing lovingly, flirting about a meeting place. It revolted me.

"I'm going to London to buy a hat," she'd say, returning glowing (almost smelling of sex), hours later, having been in the arms of her adulterer. I've hated betrayal of any kind ever since. Later, seeing the pain my father endured during a horrid divorce, I realised she was the most selfish person ever. She neither cared nor comforted the pain. I was even more confused.

Forced to move to Islington, after her marriage to Lionel Hale, I found my relationship with her broke daily into fragments of feeling unwanted and unloved. My endless tellings-off turned my brothers and sisters against me. Here comes the black sheep! As I got older, I often wanted to commit suicide, but couldn't quite do it. Mum could switch from being lovely or loving to someone, to looking at me with eyes of fury - almost hate. It gave me a chronic inferiority complex from which I have never recovered. I was twice sent to a psychiatrist, but I could never trust them enough to disclose my deep unhappiness.

Family

It is a pain of such despair
Not included in the family affair
To be forgotten is to be unnamed
Not belonging, recognised, never acclaimed
Sorrows the soul, belonging maimed,
Help me while I am remained.
Can no one hold me tight like baggage claimed?

I was saved by Granny offering "to have this dreadful girl", as it was put. My wonderful Granny changed my life. I grew in safety from being hurt. Both grandparents loved me, made me laugh and I flourished in my dancing, much to my parents' despair. They thought it was a waste of time, but Granny paid and believed in me. I got into the Royal Opera Ballet and danced at Covent Garden - oh heaven! - I'd achieved a wonderful thing.

Due to my deep insecurity, I progressed slowly with my love life. I put many a man off by being too intense and longing for a lasting relationship.

When I rang Mum to say, "I'm married!" she replied, "Oh my goodness, how awful, being married to a stockbroker!" Dad was thrilled and loved Chris, and admired what I did for him and his kids.

During married life, Mum demanded that we go over for family 'do's'. I resisted, fearful of her bossing. She was very jealous of me living by the river, in the same street where she'd grown up. "You're jolly lucky, that's where I should be", she said. She rarely came to see us, but constantly reminded me how much she enjoyed my brother's kids, and her own. She never actually listened to anything, her selfishness overruled all.

Now she's gone, I still hate what she did to me and cannot forgive her. Even more, I despise her trump card of inflicting pain through her will. I look at her photo – her smile is false - I can't see behind it. I used to hope there was love there. It doesn't exist.

I may be called a liar by my siblings (the few left), who Mum favoured and enjoyed. They took sides. My brother used to ring me up and say, "Why haven't you been to see Mum, you really ought to". I grew away from them by focussing on my own family; cherishing and loving them, creating a happy, lovingly cosy childhood for my girls and step-children. I wanted always to be there, never too busy, as my mum was, never letting them down, admiring what they did and encouraging them onwards. I love giving in every way and try desperately not to be selfish.

My mother died of colon cancer on 26 November 1999. I held her hand when she was dying and all her children were around her. My brother Jeremy organised an enormous funeral send-off and her coffin was lowered onto a narrow boat on the Islington canal at the end of her garden and chugged off to the mortuary. My mother had worked hard over the years and founded and organised a boat club in Islington Basin for the local young. It was a fitting farewell.

My poor, younger sister Tessa died in 2004 of lung cancer, aged 62. Luckily, Mum wasn't there to see her awful pain.

To Mama

Saying goodbye is the stretched hand out
The voice holding in, but wanting to shout
"I love you" – but tell me this
Why was it quite like this?
How can we ever explain
The lasting childhood pain
We never knew each other
And caused ourselves a lot of bother.
Perhaps one day we'll meet another way.

Dearest Lala

When you really became eighty
Your activities have been cheeky lately
Going off to Egypt gallantly alone
Makes you a pinnacle of the eighty-year-old zone.
You are the most wonderful special girl
Who deserves all our love in a cherishing swirl
Happy day on the unique Lala day!

5. Aunt Lavender

Lavender, born on 14 January 1920, was the youngest daughter of Granny and Grandpa Herbert, named after the film *The Lavender Hill Mob*, which starred Alec Guinness, who was a close friend of Grandpa and lived up the road. Lala (her nickname) went to boarding school when she was about 10, which she resented because her sisters stayed at home. At 16 she moved to Vienna, as a very promising student, to study under the concert pianist Karl Steiner. He fell in love with Lala, but she had to return home at 18 because of the coming War. She joined the Land Army after going to agricultural college at Plumpton, and became a prize-winning milker of cows and tractor-driver. On the outbreak of hostilities she joined the WRNS and was sent north to a Fleet Air Arm centre. As there were no men she was employed servicing torpedoes. At the end of the War she joined a Mr Gatty and began making beautiful wooden toys at Holyport.

She was courted by many young men and finally met Chris Clarke at a party. He invited her for a long walk round Richmond Park where he talked about his relatives for hours. Her only thought was, "What would he be like in bed?" as he was 10 years older, but they eventually married at St. Nicholas Church. Granny had special silk sent from Paris for her dress.

On the first night of their honeymoon all their wedding presents were stolen. Chris was already a partner of the well-known firm of Slaughter & May and eventually became senior partner. Lala had great pain at the birth of all her four children. Sadly, her eldest son Stephen, a promising law student, died after immense problems with cancer in his 30s. Lala nursed him with utter devotion over a long period.

The family bought a much-enjoyed narrow boat, and Lala and Chris had such fun cruising along some of the most difficult navigations in England. They were diligent growers of produce on their Fulham allotment and became almost self-sufficient. Lala was forever helping good causes; orphans from some unknown province or a local scrounger who kept coming back to 'borrow' money for fags or booze. She and Chris were dedicated workers for the Green Party and enrolled many new members.

After a hard life as a prisoner of war on the Burma railway, long office hours and a quiet retirement, Chris died peacefully in Lala's arms at home. Lala has just celebrated her 87th birthday and continues to astonish us all. She attends French lessons, plays the piano and is a doughty chess player. One of her greater pleasures is music: when I take her to *La Bohème* or *Madame Butterfly* she sings along to the arias, unable to contain her joy. I see her every week with a Dover sole in my hand. I love her and admire her courage and ever-happy disposition. She suffers great and continual pain in her shoulders and neck due to arthritis, but never complains.

6. *Uncle John*

Uncle John was born in 1924, the youngest of A.P.H.'s four children. He followed his father to Winchester, but although not such a brilliant classicist and having a report which once said, "Completely unable to express himself on paper", he went on to become a newspaper reporter and finally a director of public relations.

At 18 he joined up, in the Royal Navy, and had a successful War, becoming at one time the youngest lieutenant in the Navy. He sailed all over the globe, finally coming home for demob from Melbourne, Australia. He wirelessed ahead to Grandpa who met him in the *Water Gipsy* as his ship was about to dock at Tilbury. He wrote an article about his experiences in the Royal Navy and being away from the UK for two years, but it never got published. However, as a result he was asked to write a book on the Port of London for the *Britain In Pictures* series being published by Collins. This was perhaps a little unwise as the book needed a vast amount of research at the same time as John was meant to be reading for a degree in PPE at New College, Oxford. But John could never refuse a challenge and the book was published in 1947.

After Oxford, John got a job on the *Glasgow Herald* and, apart from making many life-long friends there, was able to use his position as a journalist to go round the shipyards, see over steel mills and even go down some of the Lanarkshire coal pits. In 1950 he joined the *Daily Mail* in London and, shortly after, moved to the *Daily Telegraph.* His success as a reporter did a lot for his self-confidence, which had always been fragile in the shadow of his brilliant father, but the pay was poor. He had married Gill Horrocks in 1956 and Robin, his first son, was coming along so, like many other colleagues, he decided to go into public relations and, by chance, joined Patrick Dolan's firm.

Two years later, Christie's, the fine art auctioneers, decided to open a press office and Dolan's firm was given the job. John joined the board of Christie's and over the years was able to convince what had been an old-fashioned firm to polish up their image and catch up with their rival Sotheby's.

Tragedy hit Uncle John when his much-loved wife, Gill, drowned in the Thames in 1978 whilst swimming. I was in the garden with my one-year-old Daisy, splashing in a bucket of water. Gill called from the river, "Hi Char!" swimming happily. This was the last I saw of her. Mich, her youngest son and my fond cousin, had gone indoors and an unpredictable undertow dragged Gill down. The police swarmed on the river but her body was found at low tide next day lying on a ledge on the mud. Poor John, she was such fun. We miss her dreadfully.

In 1990, when his mother moved out of her house to live with her daughter Lavender, John moved next door from Number 13 to Number 12 and lives there still. He was racing international 14ft. dinghies until 1982, when he bought his first keel boat which he raced and also took round the Mediterranean and later across the Atlantic to the Caribbean and to the east coast of America.

Now, in 2007, he has five grandchildren. I see him every week when I buy a much-enjoyed Dover sole for him. He has a lovely head of white, grey hair and a rugged brown face, lined by many windy boat trips. He's our local squire and a very popular neighbour. Aged 83, he still goes on a boat round the islands in the summer.

7. *Aunt Jocelyn*

Jocelyn, second daughter of A.P.H., grew up in a world populated with painters, writers and theatre people, and often watched rehearsals of the plays put on by her father. She married Anthony Lousada, a lawyer. After studying painting and theatre design, and bringing up four children, she joined the Royal Court Theatre in 1956.

She collaborated with George Devine, Tony Richardson, Bill Gaskill, Lindsay Anderson and John Dexter, in the emergence of a number of first performances of plays by John Arden, Arnold Wesker, John Osborne, David Storey and Samuel Beckett, where her sets were open, minimalist and enhanced the writer's work as opposed to being works of art themselves. Her designs were unique and an inspiration for many other young designers.

She also designed sets for the Metropolitan Opera House in New York, the Paris Opera House and spaces as diverse as the Ancient Stadium in Delphi and the Haymarket Theatre, Leicester.

She was a wonderful, calm and gentle person and died peacefully in May 2003, aged 86.

JULIAN HERBERT

8. *Tony Beckley* *"Chiefie"*

I remember my audition for Bernard Miles' production of *The Bedbug*. It took place in his rambling office overlooking the Thames. His lovely Mermaid Theatre was buzzing with new ideas and plays. He asked me for my thoughts on Russian writers. I didn't admit I'd never heard of Mayakovsky (author of *The Bedbug*), but diverted the easy chat to Russian ballet. I got a small part in this extraordinary production, with Joss Ackland playing the lead. The play opened with various students in bed, lounging around, discussing politics. Here, on stage, I met Tony Beckley, a strong actor with an interesting face, who had some witty, yet sardonic, lines to say.

After rehearsals one afternoon, I found myself sitting on a bench talking avidly to Tony. As we rolled along on a tide of words a friendship began. Five hours later we parted, knowing two powerful roots had planted themselves. Little did I know what a profound effect this new friend would have on my life. He decided to call me Lotte (not Charlotte any more), and in the course of time he became Chiefie.

Tony opened a door to me both emotionally and spiritually. No one has done so before or since. Our journey in fondness grew quickly, through long discussions on every aspect of life - especially childhood memories and deprivations. Tony's background was humble indeed. He lived with his single mum in a tiny flat and had to share a bed with her during the War, as bombs fell on nearby Streatham. There was little money, even though his warm-hearted mum went out to work all day.

My childhood deprivations were very different, but equally hard to understand or deal with. He was baffled that I should have been ignored for who I was. Tony had a depth I've never encountered in anyone. Getting to know him was like peeling skin after skin from an enormous onion.

He was an entirely self-taught human being in music, one of our great shared passions, and painting, as well as being a most knowledgeable reader. I'm not sure how he got to drama school except that he won a scholarship and met Sheila Hancock and Nigel Hawthorne, who became lifelong friends, and many others. He was a most talented actor, very strong (with a slightly cruel streak on occasion), and with wonderful eyes; yet he needed a lot of encouragement to strengthen his performances in *Marlowe* at Margate, *Look Back In Anger* at Croydon and a lead in the film *The Italian Job*.

Beyond this, he taught me all I know about Mahler, whose every symphony expresses such power and tragedy (his music seared our souls, especially the *adagio* movements). Tony's enthusiasm was contagious. We explored the depths of *Der Rosenkavalier* and Richard Strauss's last four songs, played at full volume in the flat he shared with Barry. The walls shook, our emotions fulfilled: Brahms broke our hearts, Mozart's genius delighted us and we relished the humour of his operas. I love Verdi operas too.

Barry Krost was Tony's agent and lover. He was an ex-hairdresser from an East End Jewish family. He adored Tony and looked after his career. We three had great fun together, although there was a time when I almost became a threat to their relationship, because Tony did seem to love being with me. We shared some visits to the theatre, where we saw John Gielgud, Lawrence Olivier and Ralph Richardson - all the greats.

Our threesome became stressed at times when I was cast as the queens' moll accompanying them to Chelsea, where they would pick up someone for the night to join their antics. Or else Barry would acquire a bit of rough for Tony to enjoy. On these occasions I was dismissed for the night to my bed-sit opposite. It was an odd life for me because I'd fallen so deeply in love with Tony. He liked the admiration and utter devotion I bestowed daily. For my part, it ended each night when his front door shut.

Tony developed a great flair for oil and gouache painting. Granny enjoyed his interest in art and became fond of him too.

He used me as a model (dressed) sometimes. I was willowy, with flowing, fair hair, and quite attractive I think in those days. Perhaps an underlying sensuality matched Tony's. Oh, how I longed to change him from being gay.

One weekend, Barry booked us to a fantastic hotel in Climping in Sussex... an Elizabethan, beamed place with huge log fires. I slept in a small room, next to their palatial, four-poster bedroom. It was a crazy weekend of grandness that Barry in particular loved, dressing for dinner and being served the best wines by a butler. On daily visits to the cool beach Tony taught me to draw charcoal pictures of breakwaters, some of which turned out rather well.

I think Tony gave me the beginning of confidence in myself - because we were happy at times. Sadly though, when things got too intense as they always did with me, because I longed for a lasting relationship, the balance shifted. Everything got a bit strained although we remained the closest friends. Sadly, Tony went to New York with Barry. At our last supper before the move, he said, "Lotte, don't hug me, I've got a lump on my leg, a sarcoma". Tragically, he died a year later in America. He was godfather to Zoë who never reaped the benefits of such a rare being. How I miss you, Chiefie.

"Chiefie"

9. *Chris*

Chris has two older sisters, Ann and Jean, and because they went to boarding school, his early childhood was quite lonely. His father was a doctor, like his forebears, and his mother was a Princess Christian nursery nurse until she gave up after marriage.

It was a fairly matter-of-fact household (perhaps because they were all in the medical profession). During the War Chris went to boarding school. Then tragedy struck - his father and a friend drowned in a sailing accident when he was 13. Of course, it had a profound effect on him and has made it hard for him to express his feelings ever since.

After school Chris did a variety of jobs; an engineering apprenticeship, National Service, engineering again, managing a granite quarry, sacked and, eventually found a job in stockbroking and has flourished ever since.

In 1963 he met and married young Suzie who was only 18. He was nine years older and together they moved into his great aunt's beautiful house in Hammersmith Terrace on the river. The aunt was a painter/etcher and used the house as a studio, coming down from her house in Enderby, Leicestershire, for artistic periods. There was a huge etching press in the garden and many of the etchings remain under the stairs, unobserved.

First, Andrew was born, to the great delight of Chris who was looking forward to fatherhood and, two years later, Sarah arrived. But then things started to go wrong for Chris - who made every effort to maintain the marriage - but Suzie rejected him and started looking outwards to other men.

As an out-of-work actress I looked after many local kids, and came on the scene babysitting. Suzie was already involved in various affairs - unbeknown to Chris. The betrayal reminded me of my mother and Lionel, and I could foresee the damage. Soon I was asked to come and help with Sunday lunch as Suzie was out at weekends, so I helped the children with activities and saw Chris become a withdrawn, anxious father. Andy was four and Sarah two. Suzie had just started an affair with Lord Valentine Thynne, of which Chris was unaware. Their relationship worsened as his hopes and efforts were rejected.

Having looked after so many local children and still out of work with a very great need of cash, to my great surprise all my neighbours bought me a secondhand, Citroen 2CV. It was a great moment to own a car. I later became a familiar sight on film sets with my flaxen hair flying out of the open roof of the car.

Chris was a fantastic father, putting his children to bed each night and reading them stories. He became a sad, enclosed person as the pedestal he had built for Suzie collapsed. I began to try and comfort him and was some help in salvaging his ruined feelings and confidence. I introduced him to the music of Faure, Mozart, Rossini and Mahler, and some opera. Verdi appealed greatly. Eventually, Chris endured the most bitter, acrimonious divorce, amid hellfire and lies from Suzie. He got well deserved care and custody of both children.

Now I really had to help as mother hen. I gave up my acting career, having just finished filming *Anne of the Thousand Days*. Stability was restored at home by my utter devotion. It was a very demanding time in my life – but somehow I'd always wanted to be needed, that suited my being. I don't know how I survived Suzie's cruel tirades.

A year later Chris proposed to me. We married very quietly in the middle of busy Hammersmith Broadway Registry Office. Best man Stefan Olszowski (Chris's best friend) and dear Granny Herbert were witnesses. Chris then went back to the city. I had to collect the kids from school, nothing very romantic.

Our love life was fantastic – as if we were made for each other. It was exciting wherever it happened. Chris grew into a happier man indeed and I was fulfilled watching him repair mentally and physically. Chris is a very honest, totally reliable man. He has an animal-like protectiveness towards his nest which provokes extreme aggression if threatened and his incredible energy seems undiminished, even at the age of 72. His great passions are FOOD, READING (anything), STEAM, MONEY, ME, SEX and MUSIC. He's a gobbler of books. His vicarious interest in English history, and that of Constantinople, the Byzantines and many other areas of civilisation, gives him a fund of knowledge.

May Poem Dedicated To You

Peace - take the juice squeezed out from a perfect summer's day
Serenity as soft in surrender as life, silk spun in privacy
The eclipse that is sheer harmony, that sets free limb upon limb in flight
Senses exploded as the pinnacle became completed in the conquering of a gifted light
I came to meet the fountain of your pressure and feel you weave my mouth into a size
Discovering the tone and texture mingling in a single stream warmed to embrace our thighs.

Food is almost sexual. He loves all aspects of preparing, cooking and eating. Sadly though, I'm not a good recipient of his dishes due to a much-damaged gut and colon problems.

Chris has always been very cautious in making decisions, whether it be buying a new cooker, marrying me or spending money on a new carpet. We've all lasted a long time. He is also a great saver of money, not a spender. When we married and had our children, I encouraged total involvement with their fun and anxieties. We've learned much together through our children and it loosened some of the trapped affections Chris has inside. I invented crazy games and dressing-up plays – he joined in the madness (despite himself) with the children.

In our first married year Chris bought a beautiful steam launch called *Victoria*. The boiler stood erect in the centre, the funnel rising through the canopy. We had many wonderful adventures on this unique vessel. Chris proudly wore a white boiler suit, wellies and huge thick gloves for stoking the boiler (it reminded him of being a stoker in the RNVR before National Service). He got carried away trying to get enough steam to create the right pressure. We'd chug peacefully along truly beautiful canals in startling sunshine or howling blizzards. I would often shiver in the tiny open cabin, watching Chris's intense delight, inhaling the steam, as we pooped the whistle going through a long tunnel or steered through the locks. Oh, how we glided serenely along on these canal sorties. Such adventures provided our only time alone together and did a lot to replenish ourselves. Andy and Sarah were away alternate weekends with their mother.

But once our own children arrived there seemed to be less time, so reluctantly Chris sold *Victoria* - little knowing we would later have great holidays on my Aunt Lala's narrow boat.

I was so excited when I became pregnant. I felt so well with the babe growing inside me. The explosion of joy I felt giving birth was a miracle (the pain forgotten). When I took the tiny babe home Andy, now 10 years, and Sarah eight, looked lovingly at the curly-haired bundle of fun taking her first gulps of fresh air, as we placed her cot in the warm June sunshine.

We had achieved something together, but even that was spoiled by Suzie sending Andy and Sarah a letter, saying, "You must hate that baby when it arrives because it doesn't belong to you". I wept when I read the letter, but Chris gave me huge support and encouragement. Later this energetic girl would bound into our bedroom at dawn, yelling, "Morning time Mummy!" bounce into bed and demand a long made-up story.

Ten-year-old Andy was becoming emotionally troubled by Suzie's behaviour. Having been at Colet Court for a year, we decided to send him to a lovely school in Somerset called Pyrland Hall where we knew the headmaster Roger Trafford. Andy settled in well and built a huge underground den in the forest, where he'd light a fire or read. Roger and his wife Cheryl built up Andy's confidence and became close friends. I am godmother to George, their youngest son.

Chris in Corfu, bottom left: playing back-gammon with Anthony (left) and David

A few years on, Chris had great anxiety with his business. He bottled up all the worry, and at times the explosive anger or frustration frightened me. I'm terrified of aggression. I didn't understand why I was being put down. It was Chris's insecurity, felt sometimes in silent mental pain, which made him fly at me. I so wish he would share problems like this and then perhaps I could comfort him. His impatience is growing as he ages. Luckily I survived difficult times by immersing myself in our children's activities when they were small. But now I'm alone.

I wish so much I could slide down and talk to the deeper Chris, but even after 35 married years, he protects himself. His sympathy also gets worn by my deep insecurity and sensitive reactions. He won't even try to understand that part of his wife. When I'm ill Chris grows silent and anxious which is sad for me. He distances himself trying to solve the health problem. I likewise feel indescribably alone.

Chris's ability for tenderness with the children when young was beautiful to see. Both Zoë and Daisy adore their Dad with an amazing devotion. They still rely upon his ideas and decisions. As for me, their interest is more transient and not without criticism unfortunately.

Alas, I'm stupid (or immature) enough to be affected a lot by Chris's changing moods. I should ignore them - but they upset me. The balance of our lives changes all the time. Our best balance is found abroad. We are much more relaxed, closer and talk more. Our small house in Corfu has brought great happiness and sharing of ideas in the glorious, slow pace of living under the sensual sun. Timeless days feed the soul richly.

A couple of years ago, Maria Bjornson, a much-loved friend and neighbour, drowned in her bath. She was a great designer of many theatre and opera sets. She'd asked Chris to accept a power of attorney over her disabled mother and left no will. Since then Chris has semi-retired from the City but has grown utterly absorbed in this new role. It's provided him with a responsible, exciting, worrying and stimulating position of managing a theatre designer's unfinished business. Unfortunately, Chris became totally involved, almost obsessed, with this when he met his co-director. On the downside, it meant I felt like a piece of lost luggage and was desperately lonely. Time passed, thank God, and we surfaced together in our own pond again. I miss having a family around a great deal, but my teaching classes keep me busy and Chris helps with my Nativity plays and the baby Jesus. I often send poems to Chris and the girls, and find poetry a true expression of my feelings. I long to find a key to unlock Chris's outer wall, so that I might creep in closer to the real him and we could know each other totally. If I could iron out his impatience and aggression he would be perfection.

Now, both in our 70s, we still share a great appetite for lots of things. We go to theatre matinee performances nearly every week and discuss the stimulation they provide. Suddenly we're sharing our time at last. While I write this autobiography Chris has become absorbed in compiling it on his word processor, helping the birth of my life story.

Above: on Rambling Rose
Right: with Dan, *one month old*

10. *Sarah*

Alas, there have been several tragedies in our family life – one of the worst was dear Sarah. How she loved my make-up stories. She was a sprightly child who I encouraged to play the piano, sing, go to ballet and cook with me. We got on very well until she went Godolphin & Latymer School at 11. Suddenly Sarah changed, by becoming bolshie and more abrupt. She told me that her friend had joined the amphetamine club at school. I balked and said, "Oh, really."

Unbeknown to us, Sarah had started glue-sniffing and smoking cigarettes at 13 years, taking glue from Chris's workroom to sniff secretly. We had no idea why her behaviour became more violent. Then she decided she wanted to run away and live with Mummy in Streatham.

By this time Suzie had married and been divorced from Lord Val Thynne (who later committed suicide in a garage). So her mother had a new lover and went out to work. Sarah returned to an empty house and became a latch-key child. Gradually, she stopped going to school while in Suzie's care.

Chris never knew and went on paying school bills. Sarah began to go on the streets and take drugs with people who seemed to drag her further into the haunts that were to destroy her. Chris was called in the middle of the night: "We've got your daughter here," by various police stations. When he got to the cell, there in the corner was a filthy, unrecognisable bundle. She was put in homes and detention centres, but always escaped. Her (once lovely) body was tattooed all over – even on her pretty face. Ears, lip, nose – all were pierced; a terrible sight of utter degradation and deterioration. It was a most harrowing experience for her father to witness this self-violation.

She slashed her wrists, contracted gonorrhoea and went to hospital several times. We both felt helpless of her ever getting well again. Luckily, Tessa Blackburn, a very dear friend, would also drive round London looking for the lost Sarah. Tessa was an immense support at this ghastly time.

Sarah had a baby daughter (by a stranger) and longed to keep it, but the child was adopted by her mother's brother and lives happily in Germany.

Tragically, Sarah took an inevitable overdose of methadone and died on 28 December 2001, aged 35. Such a sad waste of a lovely girl, driven to self-destruction.

Her funeral was very painful, especially to me. During her brother Andy's speech he spoke of everyone in her short life, but left me out completely, the one stable, loving person who'd brought her up. I was devastated by such a mean dismissal of my special role in her life.

A year later Chris and Daisy went to remember Sarah, but found Suzie had taken her ashes and scattered then at Longleat, without telling Chris. She now has a memorial plaque in St Nicholas's graveyard in Chiswick nearby.

Above: Sarah (right) with Zoë
Below: memorial cross to Sarah and Joe in St Nicholas's graveyard

Above left: Zoë as a boat lady at St Nicholas Church
Above right: aged 10
Right: opening a present

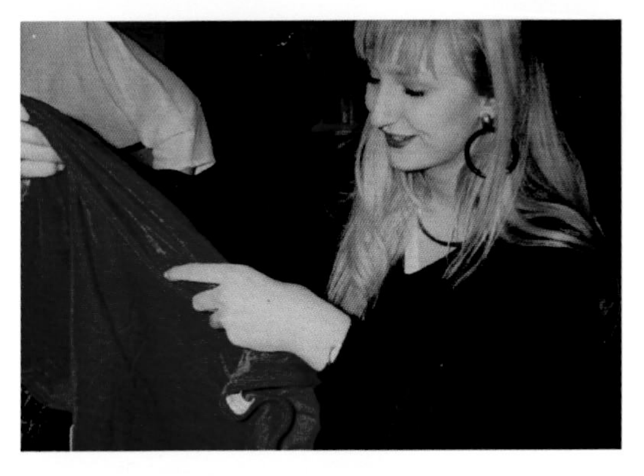

With Mimi at Daisy's wedding

11. *Zoë*

Zoë was born on 24 June 1972. I had a wonderful, happy pregnancy and enjoyed every minute of the baby's progress; playing music, singing songs and eating well to feed the little person Chris and I had made together.

As I walked along to the small Chiswick Maternity Hospital by the river, I felt excited and a little frightened. After a short labour Zoë shot out fast. During labour, Chris kept whispering, "Think of the peasants in the fields, just having babies naturally". I'm not sure if this was much comfort, but it was a miracle to give birth, unexpectedly, to a beautiful daughter. We christened her Zoë, meaning life in Greek. What a thrill to see her white, blond curls grow, to spot the first tooth and praise her first tottering steps at one year.

I had problems in breast-feeding, but was determined to give her as much goodness as possible. I remember traffic noise giving Zoë quite a start on her first journey out in the carry cot. After all that peace in the water womb, to be assaulted by blaring machines. I wanted to cover her little ears and protect her senses from the mechanical intervention. While breastfeeding in the car next to Chris one day, a large lorry hooted. We looked up to see the driver and his mate ogling rudely, and then laugh at this tiny, innocent, oblivious bundle.

I found my new role of being a mother difficult, as I had to take my step-children Sarah and Andy to school and cope with their routines. I managed it with Chris's help. Zoë was a merry little sprite; an easy, inquisitive, happy child. With a "Wake up Mum!" every morning at 5am she would bounce into bed. Andy and Sarah loved her energy. They were by now 10 and eight themselves.

Zoë loved water and invited many friends into her paddling pool or to swing like monkeys on the climbing frame. I used to play songs to her on the piano and make up stories.

She loved play group, then prep school. Concentration wasn't her main talent, she'd flit like a butterfly from one thing to another, bursting with energy and laughter. She learned swimming and ballet, but found the piano a nuisance because of the practice needed. She carved, "I hate Mummy" on the side of the piano. We all went to church and she became an acolyte at communion. Some of the girls' wonderful sayings are on page 133 at the back.

A great believer in fairies, God and Father Christmas (who used to come here every year to the children's party), Zoë once asked him for a doll's house, saying, "You can squash it down the chimney in bits – I'll catch it in the morning".

Zoë – A Poem

Our dear Zoë now you are one
First year of delight is your growing fun.
I think of you kicking inside me last year
Seeing you now, making life most dear.
You'd arrived from my womb at such high speed
A miracle of pure joy so well conceived.
Each midsummer day
We all shout hurray!

She always had lots of friends and was very happy and loving. But as teenage years arrived she was slow to develop physically. Her moods changed frequently and rebellion started intruding on our once lovely relationship. Her rudeness and resistance to anything I said started battles I hadn't expected. Chris, as usual, had the better side of her and she didn't dare be so rude.

At More House, from 11 years, she worked averagely, and yearned to be allowed more freedom like some of her high-life Chelsea friends. Thank goodness, at the time Chris was strict about evening social events. By then she had met Rami on a train who became her first boyfriend.

She was excellent at art, especially pottery. Our biggest mistake was to send her to Kingston College. It was huge and bewildering to her at first, having been at a cosy private school. Soon the madness took over, she did little study (photography and economics) and got in with a wild crowd of all sorts, smoking and even doing drugs a bit. It escalated and began to get out of control.

One morning Chris said, "Where's the car?" I didn't know either. Later, we discovered Zoë had taken it (not having passed her driving test) with her college friends and driven down to Croydon. Another time, she encouraged boys to burgle our basement. It was a wild, increasingly worrying time for us, not knowing what she'd do next. She was crazy and full of challenge to dangers unknown.

We took the girls on our usual holiday to Corfu and returned with a restless Zoë. At this time, she had no idea what she wanted to do in the future – either for a job or training – she only wanted to be independent and free. Reluctantly, we decided to arrange for her, now 18, a hopefully exciting visit to New Zealand to stay with friends and discover a new country. Of course, she took it with resentment that we were sending her away – but enjoyed the experience in some ways.

On her cross return, she said she'd quite like to take up photography or film. Finally, through a dear friend, Sheila Hancock, she got an interview on a film and became an extremely good runner (Tom Cruise said the best he'd seen). Later she did a film with Dickie Attenborough as third assistant, and was greatly admired by cast and crew. Potentially she could have become a talented director – but never stuck at this career.

She spoke to us of a new boyfriend in Shepherd's Bush, saying also, "I'm feeling broody".

We urged her, "Not yet, you've such a good career ahead of you". To our dismay, on returning from holiday, she met us on the new film set: "Guess what, I'm pregnant!" Our hearts fell to our boots. What opportunities she was turning away.

Her pregnancy became full of problems. Her womb kept losing the fluid surrounding the babe, so each week at Queen Charlotte's they X-rayed and topped up the fluid (like filling a car). Then, trouble with the baby's heartbeat led to a distressing, three-month, premature Daniel, weighing only 1lb 12oz. It was a severe trauma and poor Zoë hardly knew how to cope with the tiny fellow in an incubator who she couldn't hold or cuddle.

When I first saw him he had no eyebrows or eyelashes, and hardly any nails. The fragile form was heartbreaking. But his fighting spirit and amazing medical technology enabled him to survive (unlike my own son, who was only six weeks' premature, but died after one day). I remember being allowed to hold Daniel after about a month and felt an overwhelming love for him. He seemed lighter than even a Teddy bear.

Zoë had the exhausting role of expressing milk and bringing it into the hospital each day. Slowly he grew and gained weight. Finally, she brought Dan to their home after two months. As a mother, she found the demands quite difficult. Her boyfriend was tender to the babe, but later became violent to Zoë.

She left - it was all very alarming - and came to live with us for a bit, then moved on to a flat where Dan grew to be an alert, but demanding child. He became a burden to her social life and she felt constantly frustrated and alone. Eventually Dan started playgroup and later got into the local nursery school, so Zoë was able to see her friends and keep her social life buzzing.

A year later, she came to Corfu for a week, leaving Dan with his father's family and her life changed. Fate dealt her a lovely meeting with an Englishman who she was to fall in love with. Soon the relationship flourished and he gradually gave Zoë the security and financial stability she badly needed, and love they could share.

Mimi arrived in May 2003, an enchanting sister for Dan. Zoë's relationship with Dan is volcanic sometimes, but she seems very relaxed and happy living in great style in Corfu, a long way from her council flat.

When we meet, it's fairly casual. She seems to wear a protective shield across the real Zoë - never allowing you down to her basics, her thoughts or feelings, even her soul. She keeps her distance and will often tell me off for things I've said about Dan.

I would love to really know her again before I die. I'd love her to show feelings for Mum, to ask me questions and chat about how she is. My aching wish is to be happy and relaxed with her, but she doesn't have time yet. Perhaps these things will happen, time will tell.

Daniel, a Miracle

Three months early, little Dan arrived.
No eyelashes, so tiny, he survived
Weighing 1lb. 12ozs. piped up inside an incubator
Which became his home till some weeks later.
Through a hole I stroked his minute hand.
Zoë so strongly coped in this new land.

Luckily Dan is a fighter and now nearly 10
He adjusts to many changes now and then.
We've gone to lots of theatre since he was three
He loves the action, enthralled by fantasy.
Sometimes when he stays with us
He brings me breakfast then we discuss
People in another land or who's just scored a goal.
His sensitive spirit makes a very dear soul
Often in overdrive with perpetual chat.
I love being with my grandson, a loving chap.

He adores his little sister Mimi
Protective of her he'll always be.
Her blond curls adorn her face
Their sibling fun grows apace.

Above and below right:
Dan with Mimi
Right: Dan
Below: with Lotte

To Zoë and Daisy: Millennium Day

This time in forty years I wonder how you'll be
A mum, wife, granny who still hears
The joys of being sixty three.
I hope that humans will remain
The greatest with senses sustained.
Ability to touch, feel and talk
In places where no machine can walk.
I wish you a great millennium time
With lives fulfilled wherever you climb.

12. Daisy

Daisy was created at the right temperature level while we lay in bed watching the Derby in 1977. The previous year I bore a son Joe who sadly only lived for 24 hours. Having lost him so painfully at seven and a half months, I was desperate to conceive in one tube. Due to an earlier ectopic pregnancy, one fallopian tube had gone.

I felt wonderful during pregnancy. I played lots of soothing music so the babe could hear it while she grew inside me. Naturally I gave up smoking and ate carefully to nourish this growing miracle. Suddenly, she made movements wanting to get out early. I thought, *Oh God, not again*. The babe was nearly eight months when I went into a very painful, long labour, from 8pm to 8am, at which point the doctor decided the epidural wasn't working. Subsequently, the doctors decided the baby hadn't been able to get down the birth canal due to scar tissue from the previous operation.

The poor thing was getting distressed, pushing. Finally, they decided she must come out quickly by Caesarean. As I held her in my arms, I said to the nurse, "She's going to be a cellist - look at her wee fingers". We named her Daisy which in those days seemed odd. It suits her well. Her second name is Emerald because my mother kept insisting she be called Crystal (and we defied her control).

Daisy was an exceptional baby, calm and with a radiant smile that wrapped you in her quite beautiful presence. She didn't have any hair for a year and played Baby Jesus the following year in the first Nativity play. Her hair, when it grew, was flaxen and fell round the most innocent, gentle face. She absorbed what went on around her with big eyes. Daisy used to rush and wrap her little arms round me, saying, "I love you the whole world – more than the world".

Unfortunately, she was quite vulnerable physically and, though inoculated, she caught scarlet fever, measles, mumps, German measles and dreadful whooping cough. I remember her spending weeks in a darkened room while I coped with school runs for Zoë and the others. Discovering she was left-handed proved a difficult time at prep school, sitting next to her friend Claire who wrote right-handed. Their hands kept clashing - so sadly she moved to a solo desk.

Daisy was quite shy, unlike her gregarious sister Zoë. She started to need just one good friend who she could trust. From this pattern grew many problems and much sadness when she went to upper school. I started her on the piano at five years, which she loved, and later that year introduced her to a wonderful cello teacher called Delia Fuchs.

Daisy clearly was matched to the instrument and brought out much sensitivity in her growing talent while playing.

Clockwise from top left:
Daisy at one year old;
playing cello to the cows;
at Aylesbury; riding and with
Baby Jesus in the nativity

When she was older and played Saint-Saens' *Swan*, I lay on the floor, moved to tears. She seemed to have such soul in her music.

Both girls had fun after school dressing up with friends, in old lace petticoats and hats, making up plays in the garden by the Thames. They never watched television. Daisy's open kind of innocence was most radiant until about the age of nine when it got lost in school control and work. She flourished in Ken. Prep, winning her first carol composition. When she entered Putney High, her abilities won her a music scholarship, and she soon became leader of the Junior Orchestra, also joining a lovely choir and singing solos. I encouraged her proudly at school concerts and other school activities.

Daisy loved doing projects at school, especially about animals. I remember the whale project: driving round Hogarth roundabout, "Mummy, do whales have periods? I've got to know by tomorrow." It took many phone calls to a variety of zoos and museums to find out that they do, underwater.

Most evenings when Daisy was studying or relaxing up above us in her bedroom, Rachmaninoff would explode into the night air: the passion of the famous piano concertos raising her soul and ours to great heights. The sound rolled round her bedroom and leaked into the rest of the house. Sometimes she was exhilarated, at other times sad. How deeply those times associate with our dear girl.

Suddenly, at approximately 12 or 13, she was ill in bed when Dr Morrison announced she must go to hospital because her pee was full of sugar. Alas, in shock, we were told that Daisy was diabetic and would have to inject herself *four* times a day for life. We were shattered. Being a very brave person, she seemed to learn how, when and where to inject herself quite quickly. As a mother, I got in a panic trying to adapt her to new sugarless food and routines.

Worst of all were the hypos which neither Chris nor I knew how to deal with. A wonderful paediatrician called Dr I. Kovar managed to allay our terror of this little girl's affliction. Worse was to come a week later. Daisy was in the bath next to our bedroom, chatting to Chris who was reading on our bed next door. Suddenly Chris heard a clunk against the bath and rushed in to find Daisy unconscious, her head sliding under the water. He called me and we pulled her body out, wrapping her in a towel across the bed and dialled for an ambulance. It was February 1991.

She spent a couple of nights in the children's ward. We were summoned in to be told (quite casually): "I'm afraid Daisy has epilepsy too." They gave us a leaflet to study. God, how could this happen to our sweetest of children? The brain scan had shown discrepancies. Racked with anxiety and utter sadness, we wept all the way home.

We were to endure many anxious nights when we'd hear a thump and find Daisy fallen out of bed, shaking or semi-conscious. Sometimes we would try and pour glucose through her shut mouth and tightened jaw. It was a nightmare – how relieved we were to see her eyes stop rolling and a vague smile cross her pale face. We wrapped her in our arms, cherishing her - still trembling ourselves from the stressful happening.

This was a cruel blow for a 13-year-old to endure. She managed to cope unbelievably well at school (though she hated being cosseted and being different). There were awful times when she had a fit in front of her friends. They ran away screaming, not knowing what to do. Philosophically, she told them to put her on her side, and be quiet and calm and wait for her to recover.

Daisy did well at A' levels (and composed a wonderful piece of music for the exam). She got into St. Mary's medical school. At the interview a panels of doctors asked her, "What would you do if you had a fit while operating?"

"I'd stop, lie down and when my fit was over I'd get up and continue operating." They were spellbound. After a while, St Mary's proved too stressful, so she (reluctantly) changed to a nursing degree at Imperial College. Oh, how proud we were at the graduation at the Royal Festival Hall, watching Daisy in her mortar board and gown, with long, blonde hair flowing round a happy face.

Daisy took up – or rather won – an arduous job at St. Thomas', in the Cardiothoracic Centre for open-heart surgery. She was highly praised by various patients who felt her dedicated nursing had saved their lives. She is a born nurse (but very strict). I've been quite frightened of her orders when I've been recovering in hospital.

Years ago, we used to have the Royal School of Needlework instructor come to the house on a Saturday morning. About eight girls sewed away and learned the rare art of tapestry and other sewing methods. Daisy is a wonderful seamstress. She made her own school dresses, excellent lined curtains for her room and for ours, and several coats for herself.

The greatest day of her life arrived in May 2005. She married a lovely guy who she's known for eight years, Dr Rob Horsley. He's become a GP and they've settled in Yorkshire. The wedding was planned to such perfection. Daisy had thought and arranged every detail. Pebbles from Corfu were used as name places on each table; goldfish floated in flowered bowls.

The reception in Kew Gardens must have had God's blessing on a radiantly sunny day. I felt a little shy as mother of the bride in a big hat, walking into church – but overwhelmed with pride as Daisy took our breath away entering to the Trumpet Voluntary on Chris's arm, Rob waiting proudly for her (quaking a bit).

The wedding preparations had been undertaken with such precision. Each purple flower had to match the bridesmaids' dresses. We all argued about the menu and place settings were a nightmare. So many people didn't know each other. After a most moving wedding, a big, red, double-decker took most guests to Kew Gardens.

To Daisy

6th February 1995 - 18 today

Born a child of early spring
Age and beauty now have their fling
Your life endorsed with cherished care
We see you blossom to a person rare.
In tough time you have often shown
Great courage over sadness on your own
Our pride in you and all you do
Gives great purpose to the years in view
The first spring flowers say "Hello" to you.

Much love,
Mummy

Aged 19

During the wedding, our grandson, sitting in front, turned to me and whispered, "How long have you been married, Gran?"

"Thirty five years," I replied.

"Cor, she's been married..." he whispered to the purple bridesmaids along the pew.

When Dan and Imi, the youngest bridesmaid walked into church, close behind the bride, he turned to Imi, and said, "Gosh, this is unbelievable, pinch me to make it real!"

We've just visited Daisy and Rob in their first house in a charming, little Yorkshire village. Rob is a GP and they have now produced William Arthur, born 5th October, 2006, at 5.38am. Despite a difficult birth, Daisy is determined to have another babe soon, company for Will.

Three baby Jesus starred in my Nativity play in 2006. Will cried a bit as we sung *Away in a Manger*, but his tiny face lit up at the sound of *Jingle Bells*. It was a wonderful event, seeing Dan, Mimi, Zoë and Daisy all at the Christmas show. They all went back to their various homes for Christmas.

Daisy and Rob on their wedding day

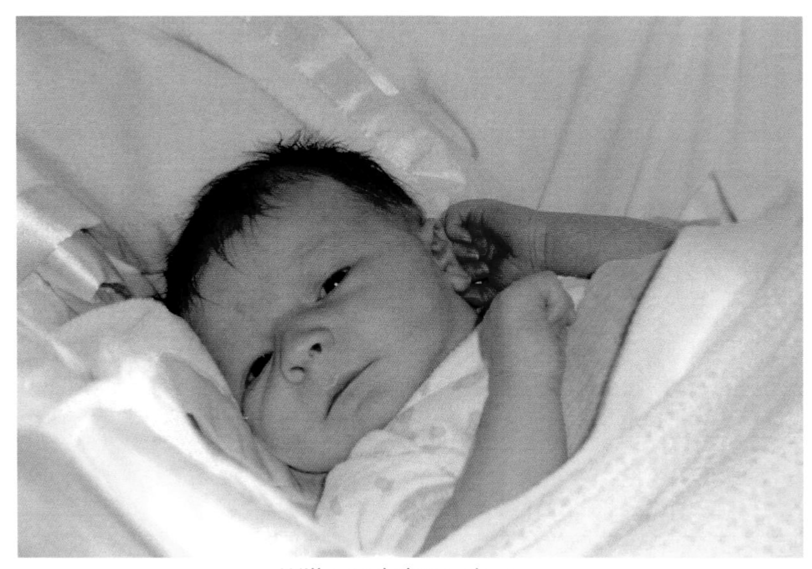

Will aged three days

William, born 5th October 2006, 5.38am

Your miracle has arrived at last
New life begins thick and fast.
The joy of your tiny bundle
Who is so tender and vulnerable
He'll soon smile and melt your heart
Or cry for hours and poo and fart
Oh what a truly happy day
To Rob and Daise we shout "Hooray!"

Aged five months

To Will

Holding you in my arms today
Was overwhelming – I had to pray.

For your wonderful arrival
Seems a cherubic miracle
So wanted and adored
You're Mum and Dad's big reward.

However far away you are
I shall think of you from afar.

A hug from Gran.

Granny in a Ploughed Field

First walk with grandson Will
The autumn air is cool and still.
Through the village I amble along
Humming him softly a lullaby song
Passing bungalows detached and prim
Beyond are fields which beckon me in.
Still sleeping Will is a little blue
An idle wind just comes through.
A rocky ride across the ploughed field
Memories return when I started to yield
To the fertile embraces amongst the hay
Deflowered long ago on a hot summer's day.
Fields and fields yawn far beyond
Low sunlight hovers and warms the bond.
I feel for nature at this magic hour
Her silence embraces such spiritual power.
Suddenly a tractor crawls over the field
Each strip he ploughs leaves rich soil to yield
The driver stares at me as my bumpy pace
Quickens across his path leaving his grumpy face
I lean over the pram to gaze at him
Sadly I'll never see Will tall and slim.
Peace has gone and the sun sinks low
Time to return to the home we know.

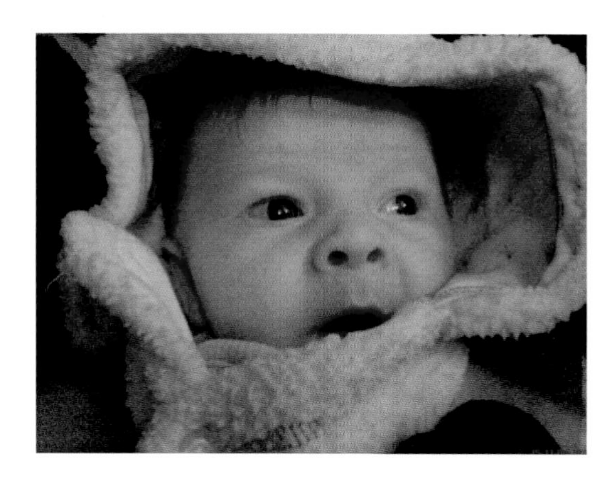

13. *Joe*

Born: 13 February 1976, 8pm
Died: 14 February am

I was so excited when I became pregnant with you. Your sister Zoë was three and a half and longed for a brother or sister. You grew peacefully inside me, despite hectic days with your stepbrother Andy and stepsister Sarah on school runs. At two months the scan gave us a scare – it didn't show you there! Were you hiding? I got very anxious – but the next visit showed you all curled up and safe. I cannot remember if I knew you were a boy or not. In those far-off days we often weren't told. I believed in the utter surprise of nature (even though I longed for a boy).

Suddenly one evening, at seven and a half to eight months, I felt some sharp pains in my stomach. Your Daddy called an ambulance, as I realised with horror the contractions had come too early. The pain worsened and I was taken *alone* by ambulance to the West Middlesex Hospital. Daddy had to stay at home with your sisters and brother, thinking I'd be back later.

I felt dreadfully alone and frightened, not wanting the contractions. Desperate for some doctor to stop them, so you could stay inside me and grow for another two months, I began screaming at them to stop you surging down. They injected me with some drug, trying to prevent you arriving. Nothing worked – in one enormous surge of pain (against my prayers for you to remain) your little form arrived.

I was exhausted and in despair – but after a few minutes the nurse gave you – my son – to me to hold. You were wrapped in a green cloth. I hardly saw your face through my tears.

"What will you call him?" asked a nurse. I thought of Chris's father who had drowned at sea when Chris was a little boy. "Joe Johnny," I said, combining our fathers' names.

I kept asking, "Is he alright?" "Yes, he's fine, just taking him to a special incubator as he's premature," came the reassuring reply. I lay emptied, strangely bereft of one who had been living and kicking inside me, someone I'd felt so strongly, who now was a much-longed-for son. I was so tired; I drifted (drugged) into an anxious oblivion.

Waiting next morning, longing to see you, I saw Daddy's solemn, sad face. My heart constricted. "I'm afraid he didn't survive." The words wailed into my guts. The terrible sadness waded into me, sobbing. Your Daddy had never seen you, nor felt you. There was silence in the little side room. I wondered where you were now. I wanted to see you.

"He was taken to Queen Charlotte's Hospital, to a special premature baby unit, because his lungs were weak," said Daddy. I began to worry that something had been seriously wrong with you, even abnormal, because I saw you so briefly. I kept asking, why, why, did you die?

The emptiness, both emotionally and physically, was devastating, but I had to go home and cope with the children, and somehow be brave, hide the sorrow and not talk about you. Daddy and I were so confused; he was incapable of thinking of burying you. I look back at this time in utter bewilderment and shock that they buried you and I *cannot* find out where. The shame haunts me. Daddy has installed a wee memorial in St. Nicolas Churchyard in your memory. The other two sons I lost, I never saw.

I think of you often, especially on 13 February, when you arrived in 1976, and the next day when you died. Daddy never wants to talk about it, which is sad. We both made you with much pleasure, I wish I'd known you, shared life with you, relished in your doings. I bet your handsome face and blond hair would have made me a proud mum.

A year after your departure, your lovely, little sister Daisy arrived, also early and with much difficulty. She has given me enormous happiness as a child and growing up, a rare person indeed.

Now, I'm growing old, I expect you would have looked after me tenderly, doing odd jobs, like your nephew Daniel. He's only 10. I'm sure bits of him are you. There is such caring in him.

To: Zoë and Daisy

Joe

February 13th 2006

Your brother Joe would have been 30 on this day
I hold within a cry for his recognition in some way,
I wonder what he would have done and been?
A writer, lawyer, actor or a raging queen,
Perhaps tall with blond, dishevelled longish hair
Laughing, loving, maybe making music for us to share.
He lived a whisper in so few hours,
He died like a puff of wind on the flowers.

Spring had come,
He had gone.

14. Jeremy
My brother

My brother Jeremy is married to a delightful, devoted American called Jean. They have two children, Megan and Jack, and live in Islington.

Jeremy was very close to my mother and during her final illness was at her side every day, helping with care, advice and encouragement as she grew weaker. He is an amazing organiser, be it a party, a funeral or a sailing club.

From an early age, when we lived in Sevenoaks, he loved racing dinghies and over the years graduated to International 14ft dinghies and finally became world champion of the class.

He started work in advertising and in 1962 joined De Beers and showed great aptitude in creating an advertising department. Like his Uncle John, he battled initially against some scepticism. However, he finally demonstrated to De Beers the benefit of a world-wide campaign to popularise diamonds in countries which had never before been great consumers, with slogans such as 'Diamonds are forever.' After 36 years with the company he has retired and now enjoys his young family.

Jeremy and Victoria

15. *Tessa*
My sister

After my sister was born on 8 February 1942, we moved from Essex to a larger house in Chipstead. Her ambition was to work in the theatre as a stage manager after training at RADA, but due to a back injury she had to give up this career. After spending some years as a secretary she decided to study sociology. Essex University was at that time a hotbed of student revolt and politics, and Tessa adopted the whole gamut. She married Victor Perkins in 1971 and had two children.

Tessa then progressed through Reading University, The Open University, Warwick University, the London School of Economics and North London Poly to Sheffield University where she met and set up house with Jill McKenna, enjoying a lovely relationship. She lectured variously on sociology, film studies, women's studies, cultural studies, communications studies and media studies.

Having such brilliant academic qualifications delighted my mother who never failed to point out the superiority of my sister's intellect over my own. She was a stubborn, heavy smoker and sadly, at 62, the inevitable happened and she died of lung cancer.

Tessa

16. *Tessa Blackburn - a Tribute to a Friend*

A giver of, and to, life, like no one else. A mother of wonderful children. The sheer energy and love of people Tessa generated was through her interest in all humanity. She shared the stimulus of music and theatre with many. Like her deep devotion to the Church and her involvement in New Bridge, the loss of her youngest daughter was a devastating loss to her soul.

Tessa's astonishing bravery was an example to us all. Her delightful accompanying every year at my children's Nativity plays gave her sense of humour time to play.

She also brought laughter to our Christmas day charades. She was the most sincere, honest, caring being I've ever known.

Tessa, you've left us a legacy of so much to think about and admire. We have shared a wonderful friendship. I cannot bear to think of this world without you – such a great loss.

Ever your friend,
With love

Loss

Never can sadness be more profound
Than an emptiness that has no sound
Such a lot gone that went before
Investment in love could cradle the sore.

17. Victoria, James and Rebecca

My mother, Crystal, married Lionel Hale, who had two lovely children, Victoria and James, from his previous marriage. They soon integrated into our expanding family. A year later, Rebecca was born.

Victoria eventually went to live in Rome with Alfredo and dear James married Hilary. They had no children, but latterly James became an author's agent having discovered Mary Wesley and other well-known authors. Hilary is prolific in many literary roles and is working for a leading firm of publishers. Tragically, James died a few years ago.

James and Hilary

18. *Monica Pudney* *"Moggie"*

While I was at boarding school during the War I remember vividly meeting an attractive woman on a horse with her two children. I was about five at the time and I jumped onto the gate as she greeted me warmly. Her name was Monica Curtis and her husband Dunstan Curtis's mother was headmistress of my vast old mansion of a boarding school. Little did I know that years later she would become my stepmother and be married to Dad for about 20 years. Monica was the seventh child of 11 children. Her wealthy Forbes family lived in America.

I remember going to Dad's second wedding in Regent's Park. As the taxi pulled up all four suspenders pinged and my nylons fell to my ankles. I was carrying two plants; my father looked askance at the mess.

Monica was a wonderful companion to Dad, taking great interest in all his poetry readings and new novels.

While working on the epic Thomas Cook film Dad developed the awful process of throat cancer. It was a slow, cruel journey, where he gradually lost his voice, became unable to swallow and had to be fed through a pipe into his stomach, with special food which Monica diligently prepared. Her devotion, care and patience were admirable and she did more nursing than most of us would be capable of. I used to be frightened of Dad's roar, but oh, how I wish he could roar now.

19. *Maria Bjornson*

One of our dearest friends and a neighbour was Maria, a flamboyant and brilliantly talented theatre designer. She used to pop in for chats, often in the evening, sometimes serious, or otherwise, and we'd share a lot of warmth, friendship, laughter and wine.

I was extremely close to her mother Mia who lived opposite. Mown down in a wheelchair accident, Mia became a prisoner inside her body: she had no speech and crushed limbs prevented any movement. Somehow our friendship survived through signals in her face and eyes.

But Maria tragically drowned in her bath on 13th December 2002. Our whole terrace froze in terrible sadness. We all miss her presence and friendship enormously.

Reflections

Poetry

I love writing poetry. It's a pouring-out of deep feelings, sad or hopeful: enjoying the innocence of children, as well as praising the beauty of nature. I feel harmonious when the words express totally how I feel. Reading poetry most days, I am greatly moved. Often the essence of a sentiment is expressed in poetic rhythm:

Verse can shoot an arrow through the heart
Or caress the buds of loving about to start.

Friendships

Friendships are founded on true trust, like an open contract of pleasure - a sharing of experiences. A true friend is one who suddenly catches one unawares by ringing up: "How are *you*, Lotte?" with genuine concern and listens to the reply.

Dusty has been a long-lasting, close friend, as was Mikki. We shared views about everything in life. Mikki, alas, died of cancer recently, having lost her husband and son shortly before. She was a rare and highly intelligent woman with a determined truth about her. We loved her dearly.

Mandy, whom I met filming, became a close and lasting friend. Caroline, who lives opposite, has shared many ups and downs with me, but her humour always flows over problems enough to solve them.

I have not seen Vanessa for some time and Lynn, who I have already mentioned, is a very dear friend. We send each other messages and letters but, alas, I don't see her often as her acting life is mostly in Los Angeles. I am very fond of dear Sheila too, who I met through Chiefie. Judy has been a true friend of many years and Tim was a great friend of my father. He lives next door and gives us acupuncture sometimes. He has a highly original collection of furniture. Elizabeth, who used to live opposite, is also a good friend and I am godmother to her lovely daughter Imi. Through teaching Ellie and Isla, their parents Jennifer and David have become good friends, despite their busy lives.

In this era of our lives I feel sad that everyone is in such a *rush*. If you can't spare the time many friendships will wither and die. We *must* make our days free to think, care and contemplate the precious moments that friendship configures. Losing a friendship is like a boat being torn from its mooring. Recently, with great sadness that has happened to me. The bewilderment – almost betrayal – hurts. But the friendship of children is safe and happy in all its stages; the progress of trust and affection grows.

Values

Living in this part of the 21st century, some alarming attitudes seem to be throttling our natural human behaviour like ivy. Our simple existence is being quashed by greed and misuse of time. The consumer gobbles everything, forgetting how to stand still or empty his soul in the peace of an outstanding silent sunset. The pace, the noise and the fumes are at fever pitch. To quote W. H. Davies:

What is this life if, full of care,
We have no time to stand and stare?

What are we rushing for? What is the ultimate pleasure or achievement in this mechanised world where everyone relies on automation and our precious, imaginative gifts are annihilated? People fill their time with bucketfuls of statements, style symbols or sheer materialistic gunge to satiate their greed and grasp more and more.

As for the state of our democracy... Well! The appalling deceit and lack of trust which government and politicians exhibit daily are no example to the young. What must a fatherless boy in Hackney think when he reads (if he can) about a married MP going off to screw another man while his wife collects the kids from school? Where are moral standards? We are being handcuffed by government over the legislation of much innocence and spontaneity which was part of childhood.

In autumn conker bashing has been banned from schools because of danger. At Christmas the innocence and wonder of Nativity plays cannot be captured on video in case a paedophile is taking the pictures. In spring, when so many children join pony clubs, new legislation says you may only groom a pony, but not look after any other animals at the club. The new laws will probably close many pony clubs. Daisy's childhood would never have been so fulfilled and passionate without them. Summer: new legislation says sun cream must be taken to school for use in playtime, but as a spray so the teacher doesn't touch the child. Winter: swimming on your back is forbidden in case you swim into someone else. Picking wild mushrooms in a forest is stealing. Arrogant, petty officials tell you it's illegal to smack your own child when it is naughty. Who will accuse you? Is there to be a big brother camera in everyone's home?

I despair at the great decline of tenderness, caring and honesty. The only possible hope is that our dear children will bring up a better generation in the future. More beauty, more silence. Happiness and peace are the qualities a child can give us totally. I hold their hands in my love for their future.

Neighbours

One of my dearest wishes would be to have all computers, TVs, telephones, mobiles and laptops turned off dead for a week, so we'd all have to speak to each other face-to-face instead. Who knows, some might find time to read a book or two, others to visit relations or friends. Letter writing would return. Everyone would communicate.

Music

Music is essential to me; I must have a daily intake to satisfy my feelings and ever-changing moods. I often hear a new piece of oboe, flute or piano music and learn again to listen and relish the experience. Music is a major part of my soul. Man hasn't made anything as beautiful or moving; it bestows tranquillity.

Shostakovich's Piano Concerto no. 2 in F Major seems to epitomise my life when I hear it; the 2nd movement depicting the patterns of all my emotions.

As a teacher of two to six-year-olds I still wonder at the joy children get from catching new songs and rhythms in the classes. They laugh and learn almost without realising. It is a contagious pleasure and uplifting for me.

I greatly miss Daisy filling our house with wonderful cello music and Beethoven sonatas on the piano. Her cello teacher, Delia, once brought 15 cellos upstairs for a marvellous concert. We moved the furniture out and the children, aged from five to 14, played as an ensemble. It was magic. I opened the windows wide so the sound reached the rowers on the Thames.

Now, several musicians from the Royal College and Royal Academy of Music regularly come and practise. Gary has been coming for several years and is now performing at the Queen Elizabeth Hall, the Wigmore Hall and throughout the world. Ben's quartet practise lovely Schubert or tangy, modern pieces upstairs. A shy Russian student, Pavel, comes all the way from East London, often bringing a singer with him.

The sound of their playing envelops the house and I do not feel alone.

Surprise Birthday Parties

I truly love giving surprises to my family and friends. For Chris's 50th I locked the downstairs bathroom to keep him from seeing the many bottles of champagne under ice in the bath. One of the girls took her dad out for a drink and they returned to a cheering house, full of his closest friends who had all brought various dishes of food. One of his greatest surprises was at his 65th, held at the local sailing club. I produced a vibrant cabaret of Lala, John, Caroline and Tessa. We had uproarious rehearsals in secret of *If I Love You* and *Pack up Your Troubles*, finishing with Caroline and Tessa singing *Hey Big Spender*. Then I brought in some of my children dressed up as honey bees. Chris was overwhelmed by the happening.

The most recent surprise was for his 70th. I hired a gallery in Kew Steam Museum (Chris is passionate about steam and the working of engines), and arranged with the curator for Chris to start the immense beam engine. The museum was filled with pulsating, hissing machines. He was thrilled, while all his friends were sitting upstairs waiting to sing to him. How should we bring Chris to the Museum without it being obvious where he was going? Daisy took him for a walk round Kew Gardens, to discuss a venue for her forthcoming marriage. Laying out the antique dinner plates, Zoë called out, "Mum, there's a good inch of soot on most of them!" As there was nowhere to wash them Pauline, who has for years organised wonderful food and birthday cakes, had to rush out and get paper plates. Her husband, Patrick, has christened, baptised, married and buried many of our family.

Chris gave me a much longed-for surprise on my 65th birthday. A horse and carriage came to the door. I was dressed in a cream dress and hat and we arrived at St Nicholas Church for a blessing of our marriage. Zoë said, "Take your glasses off, Mum, you look nicer." Entering the packed church I couldn't recognise anyone. As I left, I put on my specs to be greeted by all my family and friends who came back home to a great surprise lunch. Zoë was instrumental in finding the lovely, Indian cream dress which fitted perfectly and also in arranging the splendid horse and carriage. Clever girl.

Holidays

Some of our best family holidays took pace on *Rambling Rose*, Aunt Lala's narrow boat. She generously let us use it in all seasons. She and Christopher had designed a double bunk at the stern so that when you sat up in bed you could see the early morning mist hanging across the water, the sun sparkling on the peaceful canal under the window. Swans pecked at the porthole. I reflect with amazement how I coped on board in such cramped conditions with Andy, ten, Sarah, eight, little Zoë five and, in a carry cot, tiny Daisy, a few months old. No disposable nappies in those days, a constant string of towelling nappies hung in the cabin. Chris made us all go to the loo in the fields.

Once, in the spring, there was no hot water, no heating and it was so cold, but still an adventure. The beautiful, hidden backwaters and exquisitely peaceful canals gave great calm to our navigation. On one frightening occasion, Chris fell into a deep lock. All we could see was his arm holding the lock windlass. I cried out, fearing him to be drowning, but the children laughed.

On another occasion, as we entered Braunston Lock on the Grand Union, one of the kids steering the boat bumped against the lock wall. I was below heating a cauldron of soup which cascaded all over the floor. I rushed up, bellowing, to be met by a sea of amused tourist faces agog at my swearing. I retreated hastily while their flash bulbs popped.

The children often ran along to the next lock, the pace was so blissfully slow; all very good for the soul. When Chris gets on land after two weeks afloat, he drives us home at about 15 miles an hour. Zoë broke her ankle once and sat at the tiller, steering every day, singing and laughing as we passed other narrow boats.

One black, rainy night our boat suddenly lurched away from the bank. As we leaped out of our bunks and peered into the night we saw a herd of cows gazing at us leaning over the muddy bank. Glasses and plates were sent crashing off shelves. Chris and Andy put on wellies and, with nothing else on, went to close the sluices which had been opened to let out the flood water. What a relief it wasn't daytime.

We started going on holiday to Corfu about 25 years ago and found a tiny, uncrowded beach at Kaminaki, little realising what a future this place would have in our lives. The children loved the attractive villa while wonderful Alexandra, the owner, grew fond of us all. The warm, clear, silky sea is nectar to me and I worship the sun as it heals and relaxes my body. Both girls learnt to water ski with 'Stross', a very characterful Greek, and Anna who has become a great friend. The power that drew us back each year became strong enough to make me buy a tiny, one-bedroomed house there. It has great charm and is a haven for our elderly holidays.

Above and bottom right: hat party in Corfu. Lotte and Chris with Stross (above right)
Below left: Chris with Mimi
Bottom left: Lotte next to Mimi and other children

Venice 2001

For a birthday treat Chris took me to Venice for the first time. It was breathtaking, walking round the corner of the airport, stepping into a water bus and seeing water to the horizon. Half an hour later as we neared the San Stefano stop, I gasped at the beautiful, ancient buildings; everywhere you looked an abundance of decaying beauty. We stayed in a tiny hotel overlooking a busy square. The excitement of travelling on water buses was so unusual and everyone was so friendly. How blissful not to hear or smell any cars. We rather overdosed on churches and museums with their profusion of cupids and virgins, Madonnas and children, each one slightly different, surrounded by intricate mosaics of incredible colours. San Marco was awesome, so much opulence to absorb. It is amazing how man decorates his places of worship in shape and colour (mostly gold).

One memorable, misty, grey day we took a boat to Torcello, set in the marshes, the precursor of Venice itself. As we entered a smallish church there was an overwhelming feeling of age and tranquillity. The glorious, gold carvings each tell a story and a masterpiece of a marble floor had seen the centuries and countless feet pass. We visited Burano on the way back, a colourful island with every house painted a different colour and little canals weaving around the cobbled streets. The atmosphere of Venice and its vaults of history left me so full that it would take many months digesting all I had tasted. The magnitude and splendour remain in my mind.

St. Mark's Basilica, Venice

Car Boot Sales

I've often dragged Chris off to help me sell clothes at car boot sales. One hot sunny day a man asked me the price of several evening dresses (I thought for his girlfriend or wife). He bought some Biba blouses and short skirts... he had excellent taste. A few days later, whilst driving down Chiswick High Street, there was my Biba blouse and mini skirt walking down the street - on him! He did look pretty, but I was stunned.

Recently I put an advert in a shop to sell my black, suede, fur-lined coat. Someone called, asking the size: "Do you have a nurse's uniform or any underwear in bright colours... yes, I'm a transvestite... I'll pop round on Sunday." He didn't come.

My Transient Ischaemic Attack

Chris went sailing one weekend with John. I woke up alone and couldn't focus. My eyesight rolled across the page like a river; it was alarming because I couldn't control my vision properly. Lala took me to the eye hospital where we spent five hours, then on to Charing Cross where they told me I had had a mini stroke. It was the day Princess Diana died and I remember trying hard to see the TV. My eyes seemed awash.

After this event I went to see Mr Baker, a heart specialist, and had lots of scary tests. I was prescribed numerous pills including beta blockers to calm my fibrillations. I stopped taking these after a few weeks as I could no longer swim my usual 30 lengths and developed a truly hacking cough which remained with me for three and a half years. I continued to get chest infections, until I saw Dr Sridhar, an excellent lung specialist, who found another drug which reduced the cough. All the coughing produced some bumpy hernias.

Neurology

Shipwrecked on an island of anxiety
A lonely level of frailty
Illusions heaping confused veins to bleed
Seeming to blank out my sight and panic not to read
Worry pulsated through my stricken painful head
Eyes mottled deliriously out of control in bed.

Bees

One of Chris's hobbies is bee-keeping. The beehive is poised on the roof. A tiny, humming, open-wired box was delivered by post. The Queen bee and a few servants arrived, buzzing away. The postman was alarmed as he thrust it in my hand. I too was scared as I am allergic to bee and wasp stings.

Soon Chris was heard saying, "Must go up and see my boys in the hive." Daisy remonstrated: "They're girls, Dad!"

Busy bees at Chris's 65th

There have been many adventures and worries over the wretched things. The first time they swarmed they collected in a huge, buzzing ball under the windowsill of the house opposite. Caroline's terrified face could be seen peering through the window. Trapped inside, she called the police who sent in the council exterminators. Dead bees covered the pavement and Chris went to work next day wearing a black tie. "Has someone died?" asked his secretary.

He sometimes collects a swarm when asked by the local council. His bees have produced up to 120lbs from the one hive. Being mildly diabetic, of course, I can't taste the excellent flavour.

Looking Up Each Others' Sewers

Recently our terrace of 16 houses suffered severely blocked and flooding sewers. Everyone met to discuss their personal experiences. We looked at a closed circuit video showing each house's characterful sewer. After 41 years of neglect Thames Water has promised to clean out the sediment blocking our sewers. Perhaps they will now function better, but it's a wonderful way to start talking to your neighbours.

Tannhauser at Sadlers Wells

Dressed in a pink, diaphanous costume I put glue on the wrong side of my false eyelashes. They hung down like windscreen wipers in front of my eyes. I could see no one so fumbled my dancing like a drunken ghost.

Bathing Suits

A friend said, "Write about trying to order a bathing suit on the phone". The woman asked for my bra size. I said I didn't wear one.
"Why?"
"Because my breasts have dropped so I can't wear one."
"Where have they gone?"
"They've dropped."
"Well, you can't order a bathing suit without a bra size!"

Theatre

Returning one night from the National Theatre production of *Henry IV*, Chris and I both marvelled at the inventiveness of Nick Hytner's direction. The amount of history we learn through Shakespeare's eyes is astonishing as his characters draw us into a time years ago, when war, jealousy and ambition clashed naturally, as they do today.

Theatre is so stimulating. It takes you to another place where you think and listen for a few hours - supping up emotions highlighted with despair, beauty, sometimes joy, and such original thought about everything and everyone on earth. Very often one is stunned by extraordinary strengths or weaknesses, impressed by the creative vision, and inspired by acting deep in original conception.

Visiting the theatre many times a year, we learn about the magnitude of human beings and of their utter frailty too. The beauty of language and the sensibilities of the actors make such a valuable experience. I will be in awe of a certain performance, or even satisfied enough to feel (especially in opera or music) that it is total and complete, and you can go no further.

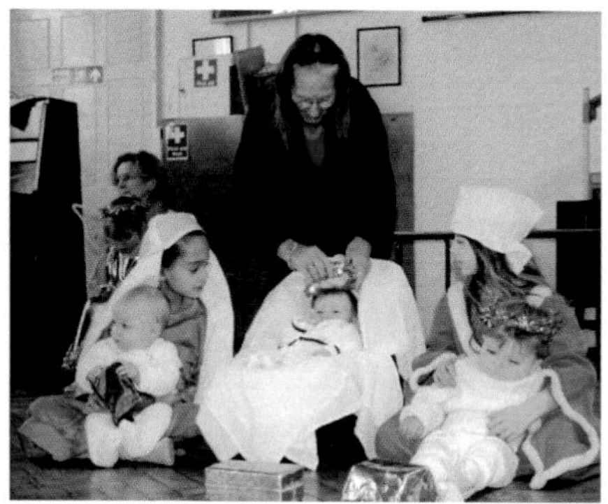

Teaching (far left) and rehearsing a Nativity with three baby Jesus: Lucy (left), Will (centre) and Doug (right)

Oh Children!

Children awaken me with their beauty and innocence. The freshness of what they see and say makes us view ourselves anew. A frank, "No, I won't!" stuns the adult. The abrupt remark is unanswerable: "What's God doing today?" or "Why has that lady got two tummies?" or "You're always saying no, no, no, why don't you say yes?" or "My dad stinks of onions!"

I love their gurgles, giggles and explosive guffaws. They cheer my ageing soul and reward me with laughter. There is such safety and pleasure in their unknowing ability to be themselves, just natural. Moments are reborn, seeing the obvious for the first time with new eyes. When teaching children I find a song will be learnt very quickly if it's funny. A sad piece will take longer to accept, they obviously don't want to be sad. Some years ago, Sarah, aged six, was so moved by the round, *"Ah poor bird, take their flight, up above the sorrow of this sad night",* set in a minor key, that it caused her to weep silently. She even asked us not to sing it on Mondays. Sadness is as contagious as laughter, especially in a singing class.

A year ago I started teaching mime to the older ones. They'd arrive bubbling after school, sing a song and then work on their mime. They loved exchanging feelings with their arms and bodies and found it very calming. Might this be a new way of calming rowdy classes at school? I most enjoy seeing a very shy, little child, blossom. Suddenly, after a term, their confidence grows and they begin to flourish. Hearing them sing their way down the street after a lesson is so rewarding.

Left: Daisy in the Quangle Wangle Hat; below: fancy dress in the garden

Emma

Watching a 6 month old baby ecstatic in a sunhat floating

Gliding in the silky sea
Daddy's arms all around me
Bobbing gently in my ring
I looked around at everything
I lift one finger to the sky
All is blue and then I cry.

Age

Sometimes I love being Granny. You're loved and wanted unconditionally by innocence. Children don't mind about the wizened face and stringy neck. They even accept my inability to run any more. "Come on Gran!" Dan shouts as I limp into the sea.

Being 70 last year, I wished that I could stop time (I didn't want to be 70, it was too old.) Alas, my body tells me each day that I'm aging. My muscles stiffen, my neck no longer swivels and it's locked in a tense stricture of pain; arthritis like a stream trickling into my joints. Wrinkles increase like a map of road junctions. My stomach, once concave when I was a ballet dancer, has scars rutted from various surgeons' knives and mole hills where the hernias jut out. My breasts, once pert and pretty, now hang low to my waist (and flap if I move fast). My hearing seems to function in one ear if I cock the other to one side. My vision relies totally on three pairs of varying glasses. Sometimes, without them, I wave to a supposed friend on a bike, their astonished face vacant in response.

Yes, I'm afraid of dying, but even more of Chris dying. I'm so anxious at present about him working in the City where a terrorist bomb could take him from me. I'm frightened of the future and what is in store as I grow more fragile. Luckily Chris has much physical strength; he seems so strong at 72. Age is cruel in the deterioration of the body.

I now suffer from dreadful cramps which wake me from 3am onwards. I jump out of bed and stretch tendons (sounding like a banshee as I cry out, "aaaaargh!"). I swim and walk the pool daily to keep loosened. Even in the freezing winter a great determination pushes me into swimming my few lengths. The aching body benefits from the exercise.

I never know what is around the corner. Oh, the awful veins that look like knotted cords down the back of my leg. I hope getting suntanned will make them invisible. Age, age and age reduces. Somehow we must retain dignity (and pride if possible), and a feeling that we matter despite being so let down by nature. It's important to feel needed and useful so that tenderness and compassion can be put to good use.

Now I'm Seventy

Do not mock when I forget
Nor can grasp the internet.
Give me more fun – enjoy me more
I'm not potty yet – but what's in store?

Trees

I often talk to trees. The big, majestic oaks are wise and old. Over the centuries they've seen so much. The beech trees shimmer in their golden, sequinned attire. Spring adorns their bare winter skeletons. Then, after an explosion of buds, new leaves gradually appear, heralding a summer of sun and storms. They laugh and bustle, getting ready for the tree ball of autumn, causing a spell of wonderment as they change gradually into ravishing gold, yellow, amber and orange, chasing the sunlight as they sway and dance. Such beauty catches the breath. Stay still Nature - let us relish the magic.

Alas, autumn fades, cruel winds strip every branch naked and the golden carpet formed beneath turns slowly into mould. Left bare, their only beauty comes when snow settles sparkling on their skeletal branches in the stark sun of winter.

Nature's Aristocracy
Trees

They stand so strong and tall
Except the wind can make them fall.
Elegance, age, wisdom and grace
Are found in no human or their place.
The growing arms of many years
Have stretched beyond where no one hears.

Photo: Vera Collingwood

Below: Winter Trees
Right: Dockey Wood, The National Trust

Romeo and Juliet

Chris took me to a glorious production of *Romeo and Juliet* at the Royal Opera House as a 70th birthday treat. All those memories of dancing there made me wish I was on stage again. Unknown to me, dear Romayne, still on stage in her 80th year, played a court lady in Act 1.

I must recall another visit to *Romeo and Juliet* at the Royal Albert Hall, attending a schools' matinee with half a dozen of my music class of five to eight-year-olds. These girls had never been to the ballet, like many others in the audience. The first comment was, "Why aren't they talking, Lotte?"

I replied, "They're talking with their bodies," and demonstrated some mime during the interval. Next, in a loud voice: "Why has that man got roses on his bottom? My daddy doesn't have a thing in front of his trousers like that."

Another voice whispered, "You see that wicked lady's hat, I'm going to make one and wear it when Mummy is nasty to me!" This vast audience was in total awe of the experience. You could hear a pin drop until Tybalt was killed at which point they cheered loudly. Romeo and Juliet kissed to more exhilarated cheering and muffled sobs accompanied the death scene. What an audience!

The Owl and the Pussycat, *with Daisy playing the guitar*

Zoë and Daisy's Quotes 1975-1980

1. 'I'm growing big, Daddy, look at my muscle sprouts!'
2. 'Ross says he's going to marry carrots, he likes them more than girls.'
3. 'I'm scoring hot!'
4. 'Do people only know you're married if you have a ring and a fat tummy?'
5. 'I've got a little bit of happiness left over from yesterday, so I'll use it up this morning.'
6. 'Perhaps when God dies Grandpa will take over and become God.'
7. 'Can I light a candle in church to the tooth fairy who gave me 10p?'
8. 'Who invented our words? God couldn't because he doesn't speak to us. Adam and Eve – did they talk?'
9. 'Of course when you're dead Mummy you won't have to think because God's up there to do it for you.'
10. 'You should believe in the Holy Ghost. He's like God with legs.'
11. (I was five months' pregnant.) 'Open your mouth wide Mummy – I'll tell you a story that the baby can hear inside you. It will hear right down there – keep your mouth open.'
12. 'Will you unlock my toes?' (Undo her shoes.)
13. (Outside an estate agent.) 'Mummy, you see that shop? That's where you buy houses. How do people take them home? Do they carry them on their backs? They must be very heavy.'
14. 'There must be a lot of lovers nearby. I can hear a lot of "Darlings" coming out of the window.'
15. 'When people fall in love do they put on their bathing suits?'
16. 'It's silly going to heaven really because you never saw what it looked like and God can change it into anything he wants.'
17. 'Poor Maffie had a helicopter in his tummy and has gone to bed.'
18. 'I'm not screaming, I'm just shouting loudly!'
19. Zoë: 'Shall I squash God?'
    Daisy: 'No, don't squash him, just love him.'
    Zoë: 'Oh good, Daisy understands God now.'
20. 'I don't want James to my party because he has tears all over his face. He's better now at school, but his tears still drop.'
21. Daisy: 'I wish you were a little bit my age then you could join in the fun I'm having.'
22. 'How do men get their seeds? How do they get in there and sow?'
23. 'When I get married you must be 89 and show your joy then you'll have lots of babies. I'm having 10.'
24. 'I've got a new friend, she's just the right texture.'

25. 'Mummy, do you know how nice you are? Better than the whole world, better than God. I love you.'
26. 'Would you like semolina?' 'Who is she?'
27. 'Don't splash darling.' 'OK little old lady!'
28. 'Look Mummy, my dressing gown is growing with me – it's growing further away from the floor.'
29. 'Stay here all the time, never go shopping, just BE here for US so we're happy.'
30. 'My headache has fallen in the river.'
31. 'Just been talking to God through a hole in the ladder. He's OK today.'
32. 'I often see granny twins, same coats, same handbags, walking along the street.'

Early Morning

"I love you the whole wide world!"
Said my radiant child her arms unfurled.
I hug what is just love in all
Its' joy of innocence and tender recall.
That vital and vulnerable child of joy
Whose senses explode and none can destroy.

Main Events

1936	15th March, birth in a clinic, Maida Vale
1937	Move to Essex
1938	13th July, birth of brother Jeremy
1941	Boarding school during the War
1942	8th February, birth of sister Tessa
1944	Move to Chipstead, Kent
1950	Leave Walthamstow Hall and start at P. Bedell's Ballet School in Kilburn
1954	Start at the Royal Ballet School
	Join Covent Garden Opera Ballet, performed *The Ring*, *Aida, Carmelites*
1958	Toured England in *Bless the Bride*
1959	Toured England in *Belle of New York*
1960	Play Alice's sister in *Alice in Wonderland* in London
1961	*The Kitchen* by Arnold Wesker, Royal Court Theatre
1962	February, meet Tony Beckley in *The Bedbug* by Mayakovsky, Mermaid Theatre
1963	Appear in *Martin Chuzzlewit*, *Silas Marner* for BBC TV
1963	The Avengers, two episodes
1964	Meet John Steiner at Peter Brook's audition for *Marat/Sade*
1965	September, John Schlesinger's film *Darling*
1966	Abortion
1966	November, help Arnold Wesker produce *The Four Seasons* with Diane Cilento and Alan Bates
1967	Play Lady Hamilton in Charles Jarrot's TV production
1967	*Dance of the Vampires*, Roman Polanski
1968	Appear in *The Possessed*, TV, and *The Saint,* with Roger Moore
1968	June, work for two weeks with Mia Farrow, helping her to acquire an English accent for J. Losey's film *Rosemary's Baby* with Liz Taylor
1969	Helped George Murcell raise funds for his Elizabethan theatre
1969	*Anne of the Thousand Days* with Richard Burton and Genevieve Bujold
1969	14th July-3rd September - meet Mandy Walker
1969	September, meet and babysit for Chris and Sue Moore's children
1971	4th June, marry Chris. Give up acting career to look after Andy & Sarah
1972	24th June give birth to Zoë at my local hospital in Chiswick
1975	Ectopic pregnancy
1976	Joe born 13th February, died on 14th February
1977	6th February, Daisy born by caesarean
1994	July, severe colostomy. In hospital for six weeks, in intensive care
1995	July, colostomy reversed
1996	16th December, birth of Daniel Moore, first grandson, 1lb 12oz
1998	30th August, mild stroke. Put on beta blockers and Warfarin
2001	28th December, Sarah Moore dies, aged 35
2003	16th April, birth of Mimi Fowler, first granddaughter
2005	Large hernia repair
2006	15th March, wonderful 70th birthday party (everyone wore hats).
2006	5th October, birth of William Arthur Horsley, second grandson, 8lb 4oz

Writing